CARL MILLES

~episodes from my life

CARL MILLES

~episodes
from my life

'EPISODES FROM MY LIFE'

Edited by Karl Axel Arvidsson
Illustrations by Georg Lagerstedt
Translation by Edwin Reffel and Sue Lidén
Editor: Rolf Milles, Lidingö Milles Rotary Club

This book is sponsored by:
Ulla and Rolf Milles
Sculptur Francis Rich, pupil of Carl Milles
The Association for the Friends of Millesgården
Ulla Fant

. ISBN 91 8702 6260
Publisher: Ehrenblad Editions AB
Riddargatan 16, 114 51 Stockholm,
Sweden, Telephone (46)-8-662 88 13,
Fax (46)-8-660 91 99

Adress to Millesgården:
Carl Milles väg 2
181 34 LIDINGÖ, Sweden
Telephone: (46)-8-731 50 60

Cover:
Photo from Falls Church Memorial, Virginia, U.S.A.
Photo by Hugh Crowder J:r,
Crowder Photos Ltd., V:a, U.S.A.

CONTENTS

7

SHORT BIOGRAPHICAL CHRONOLOGY

1875   Born on June 23 at Lagga near Uppsala,
            Sweden.

1882-92   Attended the Jacob School in Stockholm.
            Became fascinated by the sea and ships.

1892-97   Apprenticed to a cabinet maker.
            Attended night school in woodwork,
            carving and modelling.

1897-1904   Lived and worked in Paris.

1905   Married painter Olga Granner from
            Graz, Austria. Left Paris for Munich and
            then moved to Stockholm.

1906-08   Convalescence from illness (in Italy).
            Returned to Stockholm resuming work,
            handicapped by poverty and ill health.

1909	Moved into his new house in Lidingö. The beginning of Millesgården.
1908-20	Many commissions for Swedish towns and private buyers.
1920	Appointed Professor of Modelling at The Royal Academy of Art, Stockholm.
1931-51	Residential sculptor and head of the Department of Sculpture, Cranbrook Academy of Art, Bloomfield Hills, Michigan. Created a great number of large sculptures and fountains for the USA and Sweden. *Honorary American citizen.*
1951-55	Working during the winter at the American Academy in Rome. Developing his most important "sculptural" work 'Millesgården' during the summer in Lidingö.
1955	Died at his home i Lidingö, September 19th.

1982	Posthumously honored by the Swedish Council of America, with "The great Swedish Heritage Award" at a gala banquet in The Pierre Hotel, New York, in the presence of the King and Queen of Sweden.

SOME OF CARL MILLES
SCULPTURES AND FOUNTAINS
IN THE US

Going from east to west here are some examples of his extensive production.

Carl Milles (page 17)

Boston, Mass., Atlantic Ave.
  God on the Rainbow

Worchester, Mass.
  Fish Fountain and Eagle on Globe

New York, N.Y. Rockefeller Center
  Man and Nature (page 18)

Ruthsford, N.J., Forleight Dickinson University
  Genius

Philadelphia, Penn., Art Museum
  The Astronomer
  American-Swedish Historical Museum
  Swedenborg

13

Wilmington, Delaware
>   *Tercentenary Monument*   *(page 19)*

Richmond, Va., Richmond Museum,
>   *Triton Fountain*

Harrisburg, Penn., Finacial Bulding
>   *Bronze doors*   *(page 20)*

Washington DC., Hirshhorn Museum and Sculpture garden
>   *Sun Glitter*   *(page 21)*

Falls Church, Va., (outside Washington DC.),
>   *Fountain of Faith*   *(page 22, 23)*
>   *The Sun Singer*

Murrelles Inlet, South Carolina, Brookgreen Gardens,
>   *The Fountain of the Muses (Aganippe)*

Bloomfield Hills, Michigan, Cranbrook Academy of Arts,

>   *A remarkable selection of his many works
>   embellish buildings and grounds of this important
>   art center.*   *(page 24, 25)*

Minneapolis, Minn., State Highway
      Pegasus   *(page 31)*

S:t Peter, Minro, Minn., Gustavus Adolphus College
      Sun Glitter   *(page 21)*

Des Moines, Iowa
      Pegasus   *(page 31)*

Kansas City, Kansas
      St Martin Fountain

Houston, Texas
      The Tree of Paradise and The sisters

Tucson, Arizona, Tuscon Museum of Art
      Sun Glitter   *(page 21)*

Los Angeles, Cal., Costa Mesa, South Coast Plaza,
      Jonah and the Whale   *(page 32)*
      Sun Glitter   *(page 21)*

Petaluma, North San Fransisco, Cal.,
      God on the Rainbow

Seattle, Washington, Nordic Heritage Museum
      Music Playing Angels

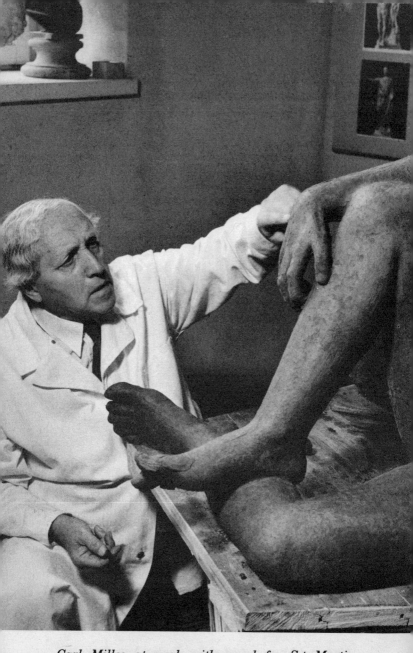

Carl Milles at work with angel for S:t Martin
Fountain, Kansas City, Kansas.

Man and Nature, Rockefeller Centre, New York, N.Y.

Tercentenary Monument, Wilmington, Delaware.

One of the Bronzdoors at Financial Bulding, Harrisburg, Penn.

Sun Glitter, Hirshhorn Museum and Sculpture garden, Washington, DC.

The Hermit, detaile of Fountain of Faith, Falls Church., (outside of Washington, DC.)

22

The Sisters, detail of Fountain of Faith, Falls Church, Va., (outside Washington, DC.)

Europe and the Bull. Cranbrook Academy of Arts, Bloomfield Hills, Mich.

Figures from the Orphus Fountain, Cranbrook Academy of Arts, Bloomfield Hills, Mich.

Diana Fountain, Art Institute, Chicago, Ill.

Dancing Girls, Missouri Botanical Garden, S:t Louis, Missouri.

Wedding of the Waters Fountain, S:t Louis, Miss.

Wedding of the Waters Fountain, S:t Louis, Miss.

Peace Indian, S:t Paul, Minnesota.

Pegasus, State Highway, Minneapolis, Minn.

Jonah and the Whale, South Coast Plaza, Los
32 Angeles, Ca.

'EPISODES FROM
MY LIFE'

by Carl Milles as he told them to the
Swedish people on Swedish Radio in
spring 1952

INTRODUCTION

Carl Milles the Swedish-American artist worked for 20 years as a resident sculptor at the Cranbrook Academy of Art, Bloomfield Hills, Michigan, near Detroit. During that time he executed many commissions among them outstanding fountains for the United States (listed earlier) as well as for Sweden. Carl Milles is today collected and represented in even more countries like Australia, Japan and Indonesia.

Fortunately we have here been able to present some of his stories which reveal the personality of the man himself. In 1952 the Swedish Radio broadcast a series of 'Carl Milles Episodes'. Milles then 77 years old, sat relaxed in his favorite chair at his home in his sculptor park Millesgården, Lidingö, and recalled episodes from bygone days.

Here we have a transcription from these broadcasts - he did not even use notes to guide him. Necessarily this translation into another language is always difficult and does not fully express his fascinating voice, delightful manner and humor. His stories are about his youth, school, and art studies in Sweden, hard years in Paris, visits to Rome and meetings with Americans in the United States.

A WEAK SCHOOLBOY

I was not such a strong child, as I was alays having trouble with my lungs and other things, asthma and so on. Anyway I tried to get into Uppsala secondary grammar school, but failed. I was ten years old then, or maybe nine. I was to take an examination for the first class and failed because I could not differentiate between Lake Vänern and Lake Vättern. In religious studies I answered crazy things and then other subjects went badly too. A teacher, whom I did not see more of than just beard and hair, almost frightened the life out of me. He also hit us wildly. So I came out of that terror after the few days of tests. At that time I was living at the house of Knut Stangenberg's mother and father in Uppsala. They were friends of my father. There for the first time in my life I met Knut Stangenberg. I was living in his room, where he painted portraits. I shall never forget what it was like there - with canvases - and how he impressed me quite incredibly, just think, being a painter - he was in the fifth class, I believe. I asked him the other day if he remembered that. No, he had forgotten, he did not remember that at all. But it does not matter. We have a tender regard for one

another, as after all we were mates once at school, although he was so much older and grander in every way.

Ever since then he has been an inspiration to me. I have always looked up to him and still look up to him to this day, a magnificent man in every way, more Swedish than most. He has always had a brilliant sense of humor. He would draw me later on in life, though always as a little fellow. My trouser buttons were never done up and my shirt always hung out somewhere. It was characteristic of me, as I had an enormous amount to do even as a boy.

Well, I then became very ill again and had to live in Stockholm, and take an examination to get into Jakob's Secondary Grammar School in Regeringsgatan. There is no building which I have hated so wholeheartedly as that one. But anyway Strindberg was a pupil there long before me. We have kept company there actually, looking at the same walls and the same dull benches. I do not know if we could have had the same teachers. Some of them were excellent of course, but some fought bravely, chasing us boys through the school rooms with some sort of cane and gave us a proper thrashing so that we started crying and screaming. We had one friend at school whose name was Westerdahl, a baker's son, who was big and strong and highly respected by the teachers. He could lift the teachers who were not too big by grabbing their shoulders and just tossing them away. He also had a wonderful sense of humor. I met him in Västerås a few years ago and he still had the same sense of humor.

At Jakob's school report cards with low marks came pouring in. I shall never forget how I was to take a card home and did not dare to show it to my father who was an excellent scholar. I was the direct opposite except when it came to those subjects which interested me. I was very good at biology, astronomy, chemistry, and physics, so I was called 'The Professor'. I always wrote Swedish so terribly badly and got the lowest grades X, Y, Z, whereas when we had tests in other subjects I got A, the highest grade. No one could understand why, but I knew very well, as I always helped my father enter records on military matters and other things, instead of studying as I should have. When I sat alone at school, I sat there dreaming that I got high grades. So I told the teachers that I believed that was the reason.

Art lessons went delightfully well. There was nothing at all wrong with them. But they were so boring, as one had to sit and draw dull cubes and uninteresting objects. It had to be very exact and correct. I have never liked that either. I believe - I have come across this through years of experience - that the more correct a work of art is the duller it is and the less it offers the viewer. When I have seen things that are unfinished I have always been delighted because the incomplete work is often that which enhances the work of art. This can be seen with Rembrandt and many other great artists who have made things using mad proportions and such. The very spirit of a work can be killed by being too terribly correct.

A GOOD TEACHER

At school I had one teacher whom I always admired. His name was Lundell. With a rucksack on his back he wandered on foot through Europe as a young man and went all the way south down to Italy and Spain. He used to tell us about it during his lessons.

There was another thing he did which amazed me too. He said, "I shall not torment you boys by reading history in the usual old way with wars and bad kings. We are probably lucky in Sweden to have had very good kings - one can see that too, of course, by reading Voltaire's description of Karl XII and from other historians who have admired the history of our little nation." He continued, "I shall write history for you boys, where I shall deal with all sorts of folk, kings and everyday people. Thanks to this history which he wrote we knew quite a lot about every conceivable personality from America, England, France and even from Asia. For example we learned about the woman Florence Nightingale, who was the first nurse to help wounded soldiers. She was with them during the Crimean War - she was a wonderful person. That was the kind of things he taught in an extremely interesting way.

Once again I was given a bad report card - it was the usual old story. I could hardly sleep! I was about to show it to Papa, when outside his bedroom door I heard him loud and clear, say to my stepmother, "It is appalling that my eldest son has to be an idiot."

Well, that affected me deeply. Papa did not understand me at the time, and I dared not show him the report card. I then went to his desk, and having helped my father so many times and seen his signature many times, I signed his name. With that done I returned to school with the report. Of course I had a bad conscience, as I had done something wrong. So I told Mr Lundell, our teacher, who had just finished his lessons, "Please Sir, may I talk to you in private? It is very important." He came and listened to me. We went into an art room which was empty, and there I told him what I had done. He looked at me very seriously and said. "Listen Carl, will you promise me never to sign another person's name on a piece of paper?" "Yes, I promise". "Shake my hand." I did so. "You must keep your promise too.

42

I shall not say a thing to anyone. I did not even notice that it was written by a different person, it was so well done. But you have given me your promise." I gave him my hand. Then he took me by the head and kissed me on the forehead and from that moment on he was one of the dearest people I met during my youth. So it continued all my life.

Many years afterwards, when I came to Stockholm from America, my schoolmates who were still alive had a party at the Grand Hotel - they were celebrating some kind of jubilee and I was invited. They had written addresses on parchment to those teachers who were still alive. I said, "Is Lundell dead?" "No, but we never liked him." "He was the only one I liked." I said. Where upon I took the train the next day. I had found out that he was living down in Småland at Unnaryd, and went there to surprise him. He certainly recognized me. He was moved and touched by my visit. He was old, like an old featherless bird. I was served a delightful dinner the first day, with soup. His eyes and nose ran and it dropped down into the soup as he sat and talked, using his hands, about everything imaginable. As I swallowed the soup, I thought to myself: If he does it, then it does not matter. I was there several days and had a glorious time.

I tried to get hold of the history textbook he had written, from which he had told us about all those remarkable people, but he did not know where it was. When he died I tried to find it, but it had disappeared.

During the time he was my teacher I read 'Tierleben' in German by the famous German author Brehm, a work eight to ten volumes thick. I enjoyed reading books like that. I was already then studying Flammarion, which I read in Swedish and then worked my way through in French.

MY FUTURE CAREER

I went as far as the fifth class, but I was never really at school all that much. Most of the time I hung around down by Slussen and the harbors of the Old Town, where I helped Captains and others. Since I did not behave in school I was sent by my father, to work as an apprentice for the wonderful old master carpenter Leon Ehrström, at Klarabergsgatan 52. I ran errands for those working in the workshop. I had to run around town picking up furniture with a handcart. I shall never forget how many people whom I had known before would not say 'hello' to me now.

My father though would always stand by my side and talk to me and ask me how I was.

When my father came home from Polacksbacken on Saturdays he would always take out marvelous art books which he had purchased. We children sat near him and learned about the Renaissance masters and others. He also introduced me to astronomy. He even taught me a little anatomy. He himself painted and not badly at all. Art was his biggest interest in life.

He had been in the war of 1870-71 and been taken prisoner. He managed to escape, with a knee riddled by bullets, back to Sweden where he became an officer. Before that he had traveled for several years across the oceans and studied by himself. He passed the entrance examination for the Latin Secondary Grammar School and took his School Certificate earlier than his school mates.

Father wrote to a man called Peter Lundblad. He was an officer who had a Swedish Institute for Physical Training in Santiago de Chile. Papa complained to him about me. He wrote back and said, "Send me the boy, I shall try to make a man out of him." He was to pay my fare from Marseille. I myself had been earning some money by working at the Technical College, so I had become a wealthy man. I had 250 - 300 crowns. I received a little money from the Technical College as I had a scholarship there. So now I was to travel to South America via Marseille.

I shall never forget when my father said goodbye to me. He called his other sons and told them to come, as Carl Emil - they called me so - was going to South America to the other side of the world. "You perhaps may never see him again, but you must swear one thing, and that is to be noble towards women." That very evening we swore bravely. Papa smiled. Since then I have visited this wonderful man Peter Lundblad in Malmö. Even though he is now very old, with bad eye sight, he still cycles during the day. When I talked to him, it was quite marvelous to hear him and see his fine noble face. His wife from Chile has learnt to speak Swedish delightfully, but makes charming mistakes at times, just like my little wife. I think it is very stimulating to hear them speak Swedish in this strange way.

But for me it was not Santiago I went to and not even Marseilles. It was Paris.

MY FRIEND O.A.

I had gone rapidly through Technical College, along with my friend Oskar Andersson. We two always hung around together. Even at that time O.A drew the most marvelous things at Technical College. I shall never forget ... Oscar was not on such good terms with the Principal Victor Adler, whom I liked very much. He was a fine and gentle man. He was actually very particular. Oscar had a strange way of treating him. He himself always did what came into his head. When Adler came into the room - with his door keys, which jangled a lot out of pure nervousness - Oscar always went and put his elbow through the window pane, so the glass shattered down on to Mäster Samuelsgatan. Adler, the principal, would disappear.

Another time Oskar did something else which could have been rather dangerous. A spring exhibition had been prepared and there stood a mass of unbaked clay models against the wall. Oscar gathered them together and crushed them to pieces all over the floor of the art room. He sprayed water on them, so that we all slipped in the wet mud. The next morning I was called into Adler. He wanted to find out from me, who had done it. Of course I knew that it was Oskar, but I said to the Principal, "I do not want to tell you who it was." He answered, "I shall give you five minutes, sit now and think about it." I sat and thought and the more I thought the more determined I was to say nothing. Then he said, "It really is a pity that such men as you and Oskar, whom I presume did it, will certainly be expelled from here before you graduate." When my minutes were up, I said to him, "If you yourself Sir, had been in the position I am in now you would never have said a word. After all a young man may make mistakes out of pure mischief or for amusement but you should not mark him for life for such a thing." He did not. He was an awfully fine man, Adler the principal.

O.A. was splendid. I shall never forget ... We had a dance every fortnight, in the so called 'Lanterninen', where the painters were. The roof of the building was entirely of glass. We danced there every fortnight and Oskar and I were lucky or unlucky enough to be in love with the same girl. We could not dance and she liked dancing. We stood there and suffered and decided to attend a dancing school in Prästgatan, in the house were Carl Larsson was born. One night as we walked home - we lived near one another - a strange question came up in the conversation. "Say, listen, how the deuce can it be? We both like this girl at Technical College and now we like this one at the dancing school too. So there we were walking along philosophizing and coming nowhere with it.

Oskar remained in Sweden and I went travelling - though I never got any further than Paris.

54

A PRIMUS STOVE IN PARIS

The first time I came to Paris I had a friend with me from Sweden, a man who was very peculiar. In a way, though, I liked him a lot. When we found a room in a little street on the top floor in the attic, I was a little surprised, as he got himself a large iron bed which filled nearly the whole of the room, so I had to lie under the sloping roof.

In that room there was one single place where I could stand upright but then I had to open a skylight in the roof. From there I could see all of Paris and that was not so bad after all. Then there were all the stars at night. I stood there dreaming halfway above the roof and halfway down in the room. But we both made up our minds to overcome the difficulties...

Being short of money we had to buy things to prepare our own meals. We in fact bought the first Primus stove, which had been introduced in France, and carried it home. We even bought a deep saucepan. We than bought a couple of bottles of milk, bread and prunes. We were quite new at cooking, you see, as with everything else. We put slices of bread in the bottom of the pan, then prunes, then slices of bread, then prunes right up to the top of the saucepan. Then having done that, we poured on the milk, put the Primus Stove on a very low light. When we poured on the milk we did not realize that it would rise! We left the meal cooking on the Primus Stove, and simply took off and went to the Louvre.

It was approximately an hour away from our home. Once there of course we forgot all about the meal cooking. This was in the morning. At four in the afternoon we suddenly heard someone say, "On ferme, on ferme" - The doors are closing, everyone must leave. Then it struck us that we had things cooking at home. We rushed home at a desperate speed as fast as we could. But when we arrived home to our little street, there were 'les Pompiers' standing with long hoses spraying the roof just exactly where we lived. We were quite horrified. We did not own many things but... We understood how it had happened. But the best thing of all was that the nice old concierge of the place came out into the street and when he saw us he said, "As you see there is a fire up in the attic. We know it started in your room. We saw you leaving

56

about ten a.m. so it was not your fault, though we do not know who did it." Well, we kept quiet, because we did not have a penny to pay for anything. We disappeared and found lodgings at another place at Rue Notre-Dame-des-Champs.

There we rented a room in a new house, on the top under the roof again, but this time we could stand upright in all four corners, so I was very satisfied with the new place. But there was no chair, nothing to sit on, and nothing to lie on except for a couple of cheap mattresses made of seaweed, which we had obtained and which a few months later were nothing but powder, because dry seaweed turns to powder after a while. We had to shake them a good deal each evening before going to bed. Then there was something terribly unpleasant about that room. It was creeping with bugs and we had to put up with that as well. We had no where else to go. Later we were obliged to leave that place too, as we could not afford the rent, and we managed somehow to get out of the house. We spoke to the concierge and to the landlord - he was very understanding as all Frenchmen are towards artists. I rented a new studio at Rue de la Grande Chaumière, the old straw-stack street that went up to Boulevard Montparnasse. But my friend from Gothenburg did not come with me but moved to something better and finer, because he had a scholarship from Stockholm and Gothenburg, and could live as a man of very fine means compared to me.

Then we parted and he went back to Sweden, despite the fact that he was a very eminent painter at the old Académie Colarossi, which was on the other side of my street. He was painting so well that he was continually awarded prizes. Nevertheless he went home to Sweden to go through the Academy of Arts and obtain state scholarships. He had been dreaming about such things. Now he has gone to Paradise and I wonder if he went there with the same feeling as a French painter, who always worked together with Daubigny. When he died he said, "I hope I shall be allowed to continue painting there as well, but I want to have Daubigny at my side."

STRINDBERG'S MADAME CHARLOTTE

One day I bought myself a book by Strindberg - 'L'Enfer', 'Inferno'. I did not know until then that I had long been living in the same street, Rue de la Grande Chaumière, where Strindberg had lived at Hotel Ulphila.

When I read that book I realized that Strindberg in his loneliness had undergone the same fate as I, when one is nervous and rather unhappy and short of money one arrives at all sorts of false notions. Strindberg and I did the same thing without knowing each other. He would never set his foot on the gap between two stones in the pavement, but jumped and balanced in order to get over those gaps and put his feet on the whole stones. I had been doing the same thing for a long time. Stepping on the gaps would have brought bad luck. And so when I read that, I went courageously out into the street and walked right on those gaps the whole day long and felt very calm afterwards.

In Rue de la Grande Chaumière there was a crèmerie which I had passed many times. There was a very peculiar poster above that little crèmerie. The poster was painted by Muscha, a Hungarian, who was very famous in Paris at the time. The poster read, "Crèmerie des artistes, la mère des artistes, Mme Charlotte". I was very curious and wondered whether I dare go in to eat there. At about that time I was working at a factory down at the Bastille, where things were cut out of wood for furniture and where the first week I earned five francs. When I had been working there a few years I was able to earn up to thirty or forty francs a day. By that time I felt quite proud and I was admired and envied by many of the old hands. One had blocks of wood sawn out by a belt saw and in that way the main form of the piece was shaped. It came over to me on a long track which was slightly greased, and then with a few cuts one was to carve in rosettes of flowers and roses and tassels. And I became so skilled at it that they literally flew out of my hands.

Enough of that, we shall return to this crèmerie. Now when I earned so much, I thought: Now I will at last go in and eat there. I entered that little crèmerie, which was completely filled with chairs and tables. I sat down at a table and was astonished to see countless pictures hanging on the walls. They hung above one another in such a way that one had to browse through the pictures so to speak. There were many by Gauguin and other famous painters. There were even some Renoirs - he was still not all that well known in Paris then. There were many other things that I observed and studied.

Suddenly there came out of the kitchen, which was behind the crèmerie, a sturdy-built handsome woman of about fifty. She called me 'jeune homme' - young man, and asked me what I would like. I wanted something to eat. "It is not time to eat yet." "Yes but you can fix something, can't you? I am so hungry." She made me an omelette. I was served by another woman Marie, who worked in the kitchen. She was very much like the first woman and spoke a similar kind of French - a rather hard kind of French. I asked her if she was German. No she was from Alsace. Madame was also from Alsace. Madame Charlotte now came out and sat down at my side to find out who I was. On hearing that I was Swedish she immediately started talking about Strindberg. He had lived at her house for three years. She owned the whole house. She was a widow, her husband had disappeared somehow, and she was living there with

63

her son, who is mentioned in 'L'Enfer'. The conversation turned to Strindberg of course, and at every meal I had at her house there was always talk of 'Straingdbair' as she called him. She narrated many odd things about 'Straingdbair'.

She told me that one morning when she came down at seven o'clock, all the tables and chairs were thrown into a corner of the crèmerie and all the saucepans from the kitchen were lying on the floor, and 'Straingdbair' was dancing a macabre dance around this ring of saucepans to conjure the evil spirits, which were in the saucepans.

He never entered through the open door. In the summer a curtain hung there, a striped one. He entered by the window, as spirits were standing at the door. Furthermore he made gold in a saucepan in the kitchen. He really did produce gold, but how, nobody knew. But gold came out of it. Into that saucepan he threw cigar and cigarette ends, buttons and all sorts of things. He never said that he threw in gold as well, but there was gold in the saucepan. One day he destroyed 'le dejeuner' for all her guests, because there was an explosion.

He also painted and she described how. He took two heavy sheets of cardboard, covered them with paint and put them together. Then he put them on the floor and stood on the sheets which then stuck together. Then he pulled them apart, and every time it was 'Storm at Sea'. She thought it was ingenious. I saw those paintings which she had saved and for me too it was 'Storm at Sea', for indeed I saw nothing but paint with many tops. I have seen those paintings at many places, even in museums. Naturally they roused great interest for it was 'Straingdbair', who had painted them in that way.

Enough of that. 'Straingdbair' had left Paris before I came there. I had my studio in the same street - it was a glass box, which had been a greenhouse previously. There I had a cat which I loved. He always snuggled up to me in my bed and lay with his little chest against my chest. The only discomfort was when he jumped in through the broken window at night, probably after having eaten a good mouse or two. I woke up sometimes as he lay sleeping with his little nose against mine. Then I would turn him in the other direction.

So that is where I lived. One Sunday Madame Charlotte came to see me. She was a jovial and handsome woman - though rather old for me. I mean I was a very young man and she was about fifty. She brought a letter in her hand and smiled. The letter was from 'Straingdbair' who was now living in

Stockholm. She gave me the letter to read, it was written in impeccable French. And in it he said that he was now living in a Nordic country, in a cold climate and among cold people. He did not like it. Apart from writing he kept himself busy with his music, but he missed Madame Charlotte enormously. He missed her so much that he felt altogether sick and very abandoned and alone. And he would very much like to have a photograph of her. So now I was to help her dress and make her look beautiful, and go with her to a photographer, a little man, who had done seven years of military service and who told us how terrible it was to return after seven years, a completely new person, who had actually forgotten the whole of his former life.

Madame invited me to her home. On every floor of the house, she had a tiny little room with a chest of drawers in each, where she kept her belongings, clothes and underwear. In the unembarrassed way French women have, she started undressing and dressed to make herself pretty. She took out all sorts of things. And then, after a few hours of discussing shawls, petticoats, dresses and everything, we went to the photographer. There we arranged her in the prettiest pose imaginable. He took countless photographs. Afterwards we returned to her place and she gave me a cup of coffee.

A week later Madame Charlotte was once more in my studio - it was again Sunday. She was smiling and looked very pleased - a new letter from 'Straingdbair'. In that letter he had written how happy he was. He loved the photo, which we had carefully selected and sent to him. He described how he took it from his bedside table in the morning, to his desk and from his desk to his bedside table at night. How beautiful she was and how he was dreaming of being with her all the time and how happy he would be if she could come to see Stockholm and see how he was living.

Now there was an animated discussion on how on earth she would be able to come to Stockholm, as she had never once been on a steamer, and she absolutely refused to sail. When I told her that there was a ferry that carried the whole train between Sassnitz and Trelleborg she did not believe it. I began to hear a lot about Madame Charlotte's feelings so I was reluctant to go there and eat. I was also reluctant to be with her, so she then came down to see me. Whenever I went there again, there was always talk of 'Straingdbair'. She had given up all thought of living alone, for she now intended to live with him. We discussed every single possibility of her being able to get to Stockholm without crossing the sea.

So time went by. One day two brothers came - Swedes - both engineers, looking for me. One is still alive and lives in Pittsburgh where he is the joint owner of a large engineering company. After visiting me the two brothers were planning to go to Madame Charlotte to eat. But before going they told me that Strindberg had become engaged to Harriet Bosse. "Listen, lads" I said to them, "Promise me one thing. Say nothing about this to her." I then told them about the letter writing and her love for Strindberg. They promised and kept their promise.

Time passed and I looked in at her place quite often, always to talk about 'Straingdbair'. Marie, who was in the kitchen, was also a part of this whole scene, but she did not like 'Straingdbair'. Then came autumn and I would leave my studio around half past six. When I passed by Madame Charlotte's little crèmerie, there she was sitting at a corner of the table, just as she always used to do when I took my meals, sitting next to me and talking of 'Straingdbair'. She now sat there dishevelled, with her clothes unbuttoned and carelessly dressed. I asked her, "Qu'avez-vous, Madame?" "What is the matter?" No answer, she did not even look up. I lifted her head and looked at her. She sat there crying. I then went out to Marie in the kitchen and asked her "What is the matter with Madame?" "Oh," she answered, "You know she is in love. Well yesterday she found out that he does not love her, because 'ce méchant Straingdbair' - that wretched Straingdbair - has gone and married Arriett de Boss in Stockholm." I had heard of that Harriet Bosse, before of course, though I had never seen her acting and now everything was spoilt for Madame.

I went on to work and was away the whole day down at the Bastille, but on returning at about eight in the evening I saw that the whole house was emptied of everything that had been there - furniture and everything. There was all sorts of rubbish in the street, there had surely been a great commotion. When I turned to a coal-seller, whom I knew very well and who lived quite nearby he said, "Yes, they have been packing the whole day long. Truck after truck has gone and Madame has gone too. She did not even give herself the time to say goodbye to us. Where she went, we do not know."

Later I heard that she had settled on the Paris-Cologne line where she owned a house. There she took care of artists who were finding it difficult to exist and who lived at her house. Not only were they given accommodation and food, she helped them in all sorts of ways, and as a result of that she became completely ruined, and died in poverty. One of my most touching experiences of unhappy love was Madame Charlotte.

CHRISTMAS AMONG THIEVES

Christmases in Paris were interesting, particularly afterwards, when one was not caught up in it all. Certainly Christmas was for me the hardest time because I never had any money, so I had to borrow in order to celebrate a little, and then had to pay it back later. But one survived that.

My sister and I used to celebrate Christmas together in all simplicity, we went as was our custom to a restaurant near the Opera. It was a Swedish restaurant run by people from Småland, the only place were one could get the rice porridge and stock fish - which we thought we absolutely must eat on that day. I mean it was nice, we did not have to have it, but it added to the feeling of Christmas Eve. We also drank a few snaps with it, before returning home. Other Christmases have been different - that one was one of the calmer Christmases.

There is another Christmas I shall never forget. At

that time through peculiar circumstances I became associated with a so called dealer, who refused to pay. He had taken work, from us sculptors, who had united, calling ourselves 'Société des artistes réalistes'. He had taken about a hundred models (casts), and ordered them from bronze founders and terracotta manufacturers. He had never paid them though, which resulted in our getting into trouble. Moreover it was forbidden to form any organization without the knowledge of the police, but we knew nothing at all about that, relying on the dealer to manage things. But he did not do that either.

All my friends fled from Paris and travelled down to the country. I alone remained. Consequently everything fell upon me without my suspecting anything. I was the one who had the responsibility, and as a result I was interrogated by the police about everything. They offered me the help of a lawyer, but I did not need one. In the end everything turned out well. In the meantime they closed my studio and sealed the lock. Thus I had to go out and find some other place to live. I was completely broke, so I went and laid down, actually threw myself on to a bench, very tired - fortunately it was a mild winter. There I fell asleep and I had on the other side a young couple who sat wrapped in a shawl. That was in the

Boulevard Montparnasse, near Brasserie Lilas, where Strindberg used to go and which he wrote about in his 'Inferno'.

I lay there on the bench, freezing a little, but fell asleep. After some time I was wakened by an old man with a white beard and white hair, who leaned over me and said, "You cannot sleep here like this, young man, come with me." I looked at him. He looked very kind and in the middle of the night he led me to 'le Quartier des Cordonniers', - the shoemakers' block - behind the Panthéon. That was actually the place where the French Revolution began. It was rather a run-down area.

He led me into a house, to a large room where eighteen people were already sleeping. I lay down on a bed on the floor - it was hot - and woke up in the morning surrounded by a whole crowd of young people who looked at me curiously. It was Christmas Day. They were really quite interesting to talk to, but I did not understand what their professions were. This old man was extremely kind. I received food and hot soup. I was allowed to join in their little games and amusements. They amazed me but one had to expect that. The remarkable thing was that as soon as I wanted to leave I was prevented. They constantly practiced all sorts of tricks, which was also quite remarkable. Soon I realized that I had come into the company of a complete little band of thieves.

The day after Christmas - or maybe it was two days after - four of them were dressed in tails and elegant clothes. They went out and disappeared, returned late at night and on the table in front of the old man they spread out a heap of jewelry and all sorts of things, including wallets, which they had managed to pickpocket, probably at the theater. Then

I was quite sure where I was. My only wish now was to get away from there. But it was a long time before I was able to leave. They went as far as to try and teach me their profession. But they were all kind, all friends and all very good to me - because they knew I was a foreigner. They were good to one another too. I must say there was a fine atmosphere there. But at last, two or three weeks later, I was on a street with them and at a moment when I was not guarded I hurried away into the night. I went back automatically to my studio and there the caretaker came to ask me where I had been. The police had come and unsealed the lock on my door so that I could enter.

It was for me a very happy moment when I could lie down in my own little studio even though I laid on the floor in a damp building which had been a greenhouse. It was in a garden. I could never undress in that studio without first turning out the light, because all the occupants of the apartment buildings surrounding it, could see me through the glass. That is where I lived for six years. In any case the old man left me in peace.

About twenty years afterwards, I was a representative for the Scandinavian countries at the Grand Palais. There I met many people from various countries representing the jury - at that time we had approximately seventy thousand paintings to go through and about five thousand statues and loads of architectural plans. It was a large international jury. After we had assembled at twelve o'clock noon we were to go out later in the afternoon and see Paris. It was arranged so that each representative had a guide. My guide was a young man who had no idea that I had been living in Paris. Even though he was from Marseille and I was from Sweden, since I had lived in Paris a long time, it was really I who took charge of him. I knew more about Paris then he did and we became good friends.

That afternoon we went to Rue de la Paix to have a drink or a coffee or whatever. When we were sitting there, suddenly there came along a white haired extremely old man with a little stick with a sharpened hook on it - in Paris such men are called 'remasseurs de mègots'. They creep between the chairs to pick up cigar stubs and cigarette butts and stuff them into a wet sack, full of tobacco, and oozing with saliva. He stopped and said, "Est-ce que ce n'est pas Milles, voyons!" "Yes, it is" I answered yet I did not recognize him. He recognized me. I was completely surprised. It was the same old man who had woken me up in the night on the boulevard twenty years or more ago. I was touched to see him. I told my friend what he had done. We then invited him to a restaurant for an enjoyable dinner together.

It was very interesting to hear about his later life. He had worked out an invention: one collected orange and lemon peels, washed them and then pressed out certain chemical substances from which he made liqueurs. He formed a company and became a very prosperous man. But he was too fond of his own liqueurs, and so that finished him again. He now went around picking up cigarette butts and cigar stubs.

I never saw him again after that evening. He told one tale after another about how the group had disbanded, spreading like seeds in the wind, trembling and afraid of showing themselves. He himself never saw any of them again. That is how life can be in a big city. I have experienced not quite the same but something similar in other cities. I have lived in so many.

AT AUGUSTE RODIN'S

We became acquainted, because my exhibit was refused at the salon Grand Palais' first vernissage. I was so disappointed that I went to the Grand Palais and destroyed all my work there. Carried out the pieces I had cut up and threw them into a large hole nearby, as they hadn't yet finished building the Grand Palais. I dumped everything into the hole. They are most probably still there today!

Rodin heard about that and came looking for me and asked if I would like to help him and work with him. I shall never forget how I heard a cab stopping outside my studio and out came a heavy little man. It was the first time I saw him. I had admired him very much ever since I had seen his Balzac at the great salon in Palais des Machines in 1897. Since then he was my idolized master, whom I never expected to meet.

Anyway it took me two years before I dared to go

and call on him. So when I finally arrived, after much hesitation, at the Rue de l'Université, I entered his studio, provided by the state - large magnificent marble blocks lay outside. According to what I had heard the state also helped him with his bronze castings. He did not receive this state support until after he was fifty, so it took a long time for him to become acknowledged. When I came in a young man asked me, "Que désirez-vous, monsieur?" To that I replied, "I would like to see Monsieur Rodin." And there he was sitting right behind me, behind a screen, scraping away at a little statuette. He asked me, "Why did you not come earlier, monsieur?" and I answered, "I was afraid to come here, you are such a great artist." He was extremely friendly. First he took me to a restaurant and then I had to follow him out to Meudon, where he lived on a hill with Clamart opposite. In the distance lay Paris - spring, summer and autumn in a wonderful haze. One could hear the noise of the city and sometimes when it was calm one heard music from Paris - it was a delightful and lovely atmosphere.

I was invited to dinner. Monsieur Rodin sat there - he had quite an imposing figure, corpulent and heavy with a large beard. He was extremely friendly, with a rather fine voice. He never really had his eyes wide open - they almost seemed shut. He drank honey-water - he and I were given a delightful meal, while Madame Rodin, sitting on my right, sat scraping away at a piece of dry meat. I offered her some of what we had, but she said in a typically french way, which I find extremely attractive on the whole, "Mais non, mon cher ami, il faut bien manger les choses d'hier." "No thank you, one must first eat the left overs from yesterday." One sees that in the whole of Europe actually, especially in the south. It is a nice custom, not to throw away and waste things.

I began my work that Sunday morning, the very first time I was there, by cleaning up his studio which was rather untidy. He was extremely pleased with that. He had almost everything there which he had exhibited in the year 1900 - in the large glass studio. In the evening when I was about to go to bed something occurred which I shall never forget. They had asked me to stay the night to save me the journey home. I had not counted on staying, and had not brought a toothbrush or nightshirt, so I was given a nightshirt - as at that time of course no one had pajamas - there were no cars either! One had candles to light one's way - those French hollow candles gave an awfully good light, but they burnt away very quickly too. Anyway they tried to find one of Monsieur Rodin's nightshirts, but they were all in the laundry, so Madame brought me one of hers with lace and things, it also was terribly long. I was very embarrassed, but I had to accept it and they laughed at me and found it most amusing.

Then we took a little walk away from his house. He had several odd small houses set on sloping terraces - it looked like a giant staircase going down into the valley - they were filled with his plaster cast collections, which he had an abundance of, all sorts - ornaments and busts of every single distinguished French sculptor. He had even collected some Gothic pieces.

There I was placed that night in a large mahogany bed, one of those huge heavy beds, where one could lie in any direction one wished. A candle was placed beside me. Monsieur went away and when he had gone I got up to close the door after him in that warm summer night. But there was no door. Well, I looked in the other direction down to the studio below where there was another house of the same kind, and there was no door there either. There were no doors anywhere. Around my bed stood six, seven, eight large statues portraying 'L'Ombre' - The Shadow - a man leaning in a very extraordinary way with large magnificent features. He had one arm hanging down and the other arm was not displayed. The founders who had molded those statues of the same man had placed them around the bed, so they all stood looking down at the person who had the pleasure of sleeping there.

Well, I laid there feeling quite lonely and hoping that the candle would burn until the sun rose again. Suddenly I heard soft steps coming closer and closer. And right after that I discovered in the doorway in the direction leading down to the next house, a huge dog standing staring at me - a Newfoundland dog. He came up to my bed, sniffed and tried to find out what strange character was there. And then he jumped up into the bed, but I got down the other side of it just as quickly. He was a really big dog, that one. I now took my candle and tried to get him out of bed, by holding the candle in front of his nose, which resulted in his licking out the flame, and there I was standing in the dark. I had to grope my way out, then walked all the way back up to Monsieur's house and rang his doorbell. Lights were lit one flight up, and out popped Monsieur Rodin's large head with his large beard and asked who was there. "C'est Milles, monsieur. There is a large dog in my bed." He laughed, came down with a new candle, followed me back and when we were there I learned to pat the dog. The dog licked my hand and we became good friends, Then Rodin left us, saying, "That dog will always sleep beside you." As a result he always slept on my bed.

However there was one snag with that delightful dog, namely that there were so many little fleas - magnificent fleas - living in his fur. Each Saturday afternoon I scrubbed him clean with soft and ordinary soap. His tail in particular was full of those small black spots. But I managed to get him decently clean and the funny thing was that he liked it.

I worked there at Rodin's periodically, but not for long periods because I could not. I had much in common with the people who worked there, fine men. There was one man I never did meet. The first time I sat at his table Rodin said to me, "Yesterday a man left me who sat in that chair who has been my secretary for a year." It was Rainer Maria Rilke.

I came into contact with him indirectly another time too. That was at a sanatorium in Switzerland where I was treated for a pulmonary hemorrhage. They placed me in a bed and the doctor who was in charge of me said, "We have not used this bed for several months. We have kept it sacred, because Rainer Maria Rilke died in this bed." It is strange that I never met him. He was in Sweden as well, you know. But I never saw him.

AT FLAMMARION'S

Flammarion was a wonderful person. When his lectures began, all the astronomers gathered around a large table a few steps higher than the audience. There were people from all over the world. I got to know a very dignified Chinese gentleman who had a costume embroidered with silk. His wonderful little wife went around in clogs and he had a little boy with him, though not at the lectures. I got to know them later. Before the lectures began telegrams were read, sent from every corner of the world about various events. People sent them to Flammarion and they were read to everyone assembled. Sometimes there would be one from Sweden - always sent in Swedish - so monsieur asked me once if people in Stockholm thought that one spoke Swedish in Paris. Eventually I became the one who would translate the telegrams from Stockholm into French, as a result I was obliged to learn terms and things within the astronomical world. In that way I came in touch with that wonderful person Flammarion, one of the liveliest and most informative men I have ever met. Whenever anyone else lectured he was hardly able to keep calm and quiet. He was so eager to inform even more. Flammarion is after all known by most educated people. He has written an infinite number of books, though he made many enemies in the world of science. He did not write with scientific exactness but mixed in a lot of astronomical romanticism, which opened people's eyes and minds to a new world. If one wished to go further, after all, one had to study it all purely scientifically. To this day I always read this sort of thing before going to bed.

I met Flammarion an infinite number of times and was in touch with him together with others, especially with Mademoiselle Klumke, an American lady who then belonged to the same French Observatory at the time. She was a delightful lecturer. She later married an astronomer. The sculpture portrait I made of her was one of my first. For me Flammarion has been among those people one must regard as 'supérieurs'. In addition to Flammarion and Rodin I also met Auguste Friedler. He was a Frenchman who lived in the French part of Switzerland. In 1900 when he came to Paris he looked me up, and returned each year. He wrote to me during a period of forty-one years. Splendid letters which I found extremely difficult to read at first. But I found a pharmacist in Rue Bréen who became so eager to read the letters, that he forgot about selling his goods, when I came in with a letter from Auguste Friedler, which he helped me to read. I learned to read them myself later.

He was a splendid fellow. He has visited us in Sweden, several time and we have travelled together a lot in the world studying art. He was a great art collector. He left everything he had bought as a gift to the Museum of Lausanne. In his old age he became very rich. He had started off empty-handed, and he gave away the whole of his gigantic fortune to help orphaned children who had lost their parents during the war. Altogether there were thousands from all nations, and he supported them in Switzerland - giving food and care and schooling during the war years. Then he lost everything he possessed. He was one of the finest people I have met.

I am always looking at the stars. I had a fine telescope but it was destroyed while I was away from Sweden. They did not know how to look after it. It had been standing outside in the yard in the rain and rough weather. But I now have another telescope, which is very good, sufficient for me. I have done this sort of thing all my life. One has such hobbies.

Another hobby of mine is history, which I have always been interested in. As I have been bedridden for such a long time with lung disease I have had time to read a lot.

A PAINT DEALER

One day when I walked to Boulevard Montparnasse
I noticed there was a new shop with a large fine
window. High up in the air on a ladder stood a man
whom I approached. He looked very odd with a very
small face and large skull with bushy red hair. He
reminded me of Strindberg. He stood painting a sign
which was above the window. There he painted the
words 'Utensiles d'artistes' - Artists' accessories. I
thought: I shall go in and buy things from this man,
when I need them. I was standing looking up at him
and smiling. He looked down at me and we smiled.
That was our first friendly meeting.

A few days afterwards I was inside his shop and
there I saw him painting a self-portrait. The air in
the shop was really awful. On the left he had his
counter. Down under the drawers a bitch was living
with her seven puppies. Further away in the shop - it
was a really tiny little shop - behind a screen was a

large mahogany bed in which a madonna sat with her three children, watching a little stove, on which a 'Pot au jus' -saucepan with bouillon - was bubbling. It was very smokey in there as he smoked French cigarettes - Caporal. He invited me to sit down. From the ceiling hung all the various things an artist might need. In the windows were tools for sculptors. There was drawing paper and all sorts of things for painting, paint, brushes, etc. I was given coffee. I got hold of a mandolin, which I was quite good at playing at the time, and afterwards a guitar too. We sat there playing and singing French songs. I still know some of them to this day. We had a splendid time.

The next time I came, he hurried over to the window, out through the door, pulled down the iron shutters, although it was only three o'clock, and then he said, "Well Carl now we shall play and sing. I could not care less about the customers." We did just that and the customers hammered on the door and wanted to come in, but it was in vain. He did not go and open the door. He wanted to enjoy himself. It happened once or twice again, till I thought. "I cannot come and visit this fellow until late in the evening". That is what I did and we be became very good friends.

Then as luck would have it, he let me see the drawings he made. He made delightful ones for Guy de Maupassant's stories. I do not want to tell his surname, but his first name was Georges. They were the most original drawings I have seen, wonderful! When I called him 'grand artiste' he replied, "C'est pas moi, vous êtes un bon artiste, mon cher, mais moi, je suis commercant." - Not me, you are a good artist, I am nothing more than a businessman. He was very modest. We saw a great deal of each other until late winter. Then he came to me and said, "Would you help me to move, Charles?" - as they called me there. I said: "Yes, what shall we do?" "Well, we can hire a couple of wheelbarrows and then move everything that is in the shop. It has to be done before six o'clock tomorrow. The next morning the shop must be completely empty." The family disappeared, and the bitch with her puppies, which had grown quite big disappeared. He himself disappeared too. Everything was gone. We had moved the whole night long. He had evidently gone bankrupt. But we took care of all his possessions and put them in my studio, which was now full to overflowing with all sorts of things. In that way I got a fine bed to lie on. I had all his boxes, paints and drawings, so I began to experiment to draw with color and paint.

He had completely disappeared. Winter passed and

spring came. In the spring when the time came to submit things to the Grand Palais Salon, I mounted his drawings on stronger cardboard. Then I took them to the salon, submitted them there among other exhibitors, wrote his name with my name underneath and then I wondered what would happen. A few days afterwards, in sunshine and fine weather there was a knock at my door, and there he was, Georges. I was almost terrified at what I had done and looked at him. He looked healthy and happy, he had been living in Normandy. At the same time as he stood there, along came a young boy with a telegram, 'un petit bleu'. It was addressed to him, at my address. I handed it to him. He read it, understood nothing and I did not grasp it until I read it myself. In it he was invited to go to the largest publisher of books in France, in Boulevard St. Germain. They wanted to meet him as soon as possible.

All right, then I told my friend Georges what I had done. It was just as if I had let a bomb drop. He got furious, jumped and ran around and was shocked at my having dared to do such a thing. All at once he stopped dead, stood looking at me and smiled a moment, taking my head in his hands he kissed me on the forehead and went away. In the evening, late at about ten o'clock, he came dancing into the little restaurant - at Madame Charlotte's - and told us he had been given work for ten years ahead and an excellent pay. He moved to the Étoile to live. Later he met with a accident and died from it. I never saw him again.

To conclude this story about Georges, it so happened that once in America I was sitting telling this to some friends, when one of them Mr George Booth, founder of the Art Academy at Cranbrook, got up and fetched from his immense library a book with those illustrations. So they were all able to see them in black and white. They were all extremely enthusiastic about Georges' drawings.

THE OLD RAG-WOMEN'S DOWRY

In the street where I lived, in the Rue de la Grande Chaumière, every morning at half past six - when I left for work at a workshop down towards the Bastille - an old woman used to sit there, leaning against the stone wall on those many cold winter mornings as she had done for many a year. I always used to ask her in on Saturday mornings and we made cocoa and I had bread which we ate together. But she was so dirty and disgusting. The dirt hung in her tangled hair, her hands were unclean. She often used to sit scraping away at some old chop-bones with a broken table knife. From these chop-bones she got a little nourishment and it seemed to be all the food she had. During the daytime I never saw her, only early in the morning in fog and damp, cold and bad weather. She was always patient and always friendly, though she had a harsh, rather unpleasant voice. But this is easily explained, of course, when one lives such a life.

She used to stand with her sack which was brown and greasy, waiting for a man who came along with a dog and a wheelbarrow. There were a few bins which she filled from her sack and she got a few centimes for that.

Well now, every Saturday morning for several years I had continued to give her cocoa so that we became very good friends. I never found out who she was or where she came from, nothing. One day, after six years, she asked me if I wanted to go to a wedding. I asked her, "Are you getting married, Madame?" "No, not me but I have a daughter who is going to marry a young doctor." I was so surprised. I promised to come, dressed in the finest rags I had and there I was on the night of the wedding at her home, where I met a charming girl who was her daughter, a young man who was extremely pleasant - the doctor - a priest and a few other friends. It was a delightful supper. The priest made a speech. The old lady herself, whom I had never seen other than dirty and unkept, was dressed in white and had washed - her daughter had helped her. We were served very good food, cooked by her daughter. There we sat, surprised as I was. But I became even more surprised over what then happened.

After we had eaten and talked, and some beautiful

songs had been sung, the bride's mother took out a little envelope which she had hidden in her bosom. She did not open the envelope but gave it to her daughter to open. She took out a check for forty thousand francs. Everyone was amazed. I asked her afterwards, "How were you able to do that, Madame?" "Well you see I have been very fortunate. I have been lucky, as I have found the most splendid books in those dust bins sometimes. I sold them. I have even found jewels. I sold everything and over the years it has added up to this sum which I gave my daughter as her dowry. It is customary for all mothers and fathers in France to do so."

MEETING WITH A STRANGER
AND SOMEONE BEING CRUEL TO
ANIMALS

One night I came home to my little studio. I had my
old bed on the damp floor - in the greenhouse, where
I lived with my little cat, who later on became my
sister's delight. When I arrived there, the door was
open, unlocked. When I entered, I saw in the dark a
man lying on my bed, hunched up. I saw nothing else
but his outlines, his face I hardly saw, for there was
hardly any face - it was just beard and hair - with a
little white mark around his eyes. I did not want to
disturb him. I was tired and I thought it was rather
sinister. I sat down on a chair, to wait for him to
wake up. He slept for one and a half hours, wakened,
and looked at me. The only thing he said when he
saw me sitting there was: "J'ai faim." - "I am hungry."
Then I answered him, "Yes, so am I. But I have a
hundred sous - five francs - in my pocket. Come with
me and we shall see if we can find some late night

restaurant, where we can get some food." We set off together with that purpose, without saying a word. We ate well, both of us for five francs, not a word was spoken between us, and when he left me that night, he did not even say Thank you!

Later, several months afterwards, I was out walking with my sister Ruth one Sunday morning in Boulevard St. Michel. There was something there that caught my attention. It was a driver who maltreated his horse in the most unpleasant manner. I lost my head completely and rushed up to the wretched man, who must have been drunk. Actually one never saw drunk men in Paris, except for Scandinavians and Englishmen. But this was a

Frenchman and he was dreadful to his horse, so I rushed up to him. Consequently there was a furious fight between him and me. My sister started crying and shouting for help. But he was stronger than me and bigger and managed to get me up into his cab. Where he intended to take me, I did not know, and people started to gather around me, calling me 'sale Anglais' - damned Englishman - the English had a bad reputation at that time in France, as a result of the Boer War. I tried to get away from the cab. The police came. But at the same time a fine old gentleman came along, and he had his daughter - a young girl - at his side. He came forward and said to the police, "We Frenchmen have to learn how to treat animals from foreigners. I am following this man to the police station."

The police too got up into the cab and we drove to the police station. For treating a Frenchman in that way I had to stay there the whole day. But in the evening the charming old man came and bailed me out. It cost him twenty francs. Inside - in the room where I was locked up with a whole crowd of strange characters - along came the man who had slept in my bed that night. He came forward and asked me what mischief I had been up to, since I had got myself locked up!

A BOYISH PRANK

One Saturday night I was going to go down town. I was alone and going to Duval to have something to eat. For only two francs one could eat extremely well in those days - a delicious dinner. Otherwise I used to dine at a restaurant in Avenue de Maine, where one paid twenty-five centimes for a complete meal, including wine, bread, soup, meat and a dessert. In the meat would be found some cats' whiskers and cats' claws and all sorts of mysterious things imaginable, but one ate nevertheless. One was young and hungry and learned not to be particular, but gave one's five centimes in tips - the waiter was extremely grateful for that.

Now I was going to Duval, but what happened before I got there? Well, the Duval lay in Avenue de l'Opéra... There all of a sudden I caught sight of an elderly couple, he in a long frock coat and she in a long gown, which trailed along the street - they were

walking arm in arm. A typical charming French couple who walked along in the direction of the Avenue de l'Opéra. Suddenly we heard money chinking on the street. They stopped dead and immediately she said to him, "Have you dropped your money?" "I do not know really," he said, feeling to see if he had, and found his purse still in his pocket. But they were positive they had heard money chinking. Economical as the French are, they stopped and started searching. Since they found nothing and as the sun was setting they hurried on. Suddenly they heard the chinking of money again. It was just as they passed the Gambetta-Monument and were about to walk into the Avenue de l'Opéra that this happened. I started wondering too. I had of course no money that I could have dropped, but anyway I was curious and helped them to look when they dropped their money the second time. She quite lost her temper at him. "If you go on dropping your money like this we cannot go and dine, and we cannot go to the theater either", she said. "Yes, but my dearest", he said and his face was pale between his black beard and top hat, "I have no loose change, so I can hardly drop any." "Yes, but you must have put some money in one of your pockets. Look if you did!".

He started searching through all his pockets, but then I noticed two young men - more likely boys - approaching with matches and they asked, "Are you looking for something?" "Yes, my husband has dropped his money." They searched with countless matches and found nothing. So they walked on. Then for the third time we heard the chink of coins. I became suspicious of those boys, as I had noticed they were shaking with laughter and trying to conceal the fact. Then they came once more with matches but still there was no money to be found. The fourth time I saw everything. The boys had those copper coins with holes in, such as one often sees in France. They had them tied together and fastened them to a string. They were amusing themselves by going out in the evenings and fooling people into believing that they had dropped money. A delightful French joke.

THE CANDLE IN RUE BONAPARTE

The story I am about to tell took place the day after I had become a wealthy man. I was selling enough to make a living, selling at the Salon. The art dealers had their eyes on me, were buying from me and my sister. I will never forget one evening when the idea came into my head that I should go out for a while. I put a large candle into my pocket and went down to Rue Bonaparte which passes École des Beaux Arts, one of the most difficult places for traffic in Paris. Everyone had to take that route across the Seine. On reaching that street, right in front of the Academy of Arts, I lit my candle and walked to the middle of the road, where all the buses passed. I chose a moment when there was no traffic. I lit the candle, held it upside down, letting the wax drop onto the cement, turned the candle the right way up pressing it into the ground and held it there for a second or two. The candle stood there alight. There was no wind. It was

111

calm and unusually quite. Then I squeezed myself into a sort of niche, where two houses met. There I squeezed myself in, to watch and see what would happen. It was very strange. First a bus came along with a team of five horses, carrying a great load of people - the driver steered the horses carefully around the candle and made the sign of the cross with his whip. Then a bus from the other direction came, and exactly the same thing occurred. Cabs came along, stopped for a moment and drove on. Everyone made the sign of the cross. Many people came by, 'Arm umschlungen', as the Germans say, with their arms around one another's waist, they stopped and talked about the candle. There were constantly new people going up to the candle. They looked as if they were saying a little prayer. I stood there absolutely fascinated. I saw old women standing there a long time, until they had to make way for the traffic. It took a long time, an hour and a half approximately, for the flame to expire in the very last flare. Then I went home to bed. At that time I was living in Rue Freyer, up by Rue Vaugirard.

Many, many years later, about twenty years later, I met a lady at a dinner held here in Sweden at Carl G Laurin's house. This lady was an American from Baltimore, and when we shook hands she said, "I

have seen you before, Mr Milles. You lived at Rue Freyer, number nine. One day I saw you leaving, and I walked behind you the whole time until you reached Rue Bonaporte, There you lit a candle and placed it in the middle of the street, I wondered why you did this. You went to stand up against the wall of a house and just stood there observing. I went to stand by another wall opposite, just to watch you. For a long time I had wanted to get to know you. My mother and I were living in the same studio block. I stood there right up until the moment you went home, then I went home too." I never met that lady again. That is how it is in a large city - you meet under peculiar circumstances but never get to know one another.

IN THE CLAQUE OF THE GRAND OPERA

In Paris I got to know a man called Georges Lalanne. I thought he was old, as he was fifty. He heard that I was passionately fond of music - I did after all have an old fiddle, which sounded awful, or was it me that played so awful. I had a flute, an ocarina, and a little accordion, but I did not have the time to play in earnest, so nothing ever became of it. Since he was in the claque of the Opera, he enticed me in there. One got to sit in the best seats, two by two, and follow the signals of a little stick which appeared in the orchestra. When we saw it come up we were to applaud. We were a group of sixty men, all the others were grey-haired old artists, who were short of cash, but loved music. I was given Saturday to prepare myself, and I was the only young man there and the only foreigner.

I shall never forget my first evening when my

friend Georges Lalanne took me to a little restaurant behind the Opera. There, underground, in a little cavern we met. They served us as much champagne as we wished and there was no lack of drinking, so we were in good spirits. When it was time to go to the Opera we were given small brass discs with our seat numbers on, and we then went through a cellar and came up into the interior of the Opera. We came up first into the engine-room and then went down the two side stairs. I often had my friend Lalanne at my side, but we were always to change places, so that no one recognized us. One was always to wear a top hat and to be dressed in fine clothes, to mingle with the audience. I have always obstinately adhered to the opinion that since I was an artist, I would never purchase a top hat, so every Saturday I borrowed one - sometimes it was too large and sometimes too small. I felt that the whole of Paris was looking at me, sitting up there on the top of the bus en route to the Opera. For either the silk hat slipped down over my ears, or else there was no room for it on my head.

Anyway when we came up from below to the grand salon of the Paris Opera, women were there dusting the balustrades in front of the velvet clad balconies and the dust of course rose sky-high. At that time there were still no vacuum-cleaners and over the whole of this gigantic salon shone only one 'bec de gas' - one single flame. When we had seen where we were to sit, we went out to the main entrance, and there in the foyer we mingled with the audience. After that we went and sat down, and followed the stick. It was a little ebony stick, with which the leader indicated when we were to applaud. Gradually, during all those seven years that I frequented the place - every Saturday - I became very well acquainted with the operas. I knew them partly by heart and enjoyed myself, and was happy to be able to be there. I never missed a Saturday evening.

But finally I became a little critical and a little particular. I noticed that one lady could not sing properly and I absolutely refused to applaud. I sat with my hands in my lap. The boss of the claque was sitting on my right - I sat stubbornly keeping my hands down. When it was all over that night he said to me, "Charles, this will not do, the others saw that you were not applauding. So your time is up. But come again next Saturday and we shall have a nice party for you. We have had terribly good fun together."

Next Saturday I came again, and afterwards there was a delightful little party with music. That night they gave Offenbach's 'Orpheus in the Underworld'.

I shall never forget when we came out in the evening, on our way to another place for a meal, with those aged French men. It was as cordial and marvelous as anything could be. Most of those who had gone to the Opera to listen, danced - they were dancing and signing tunes by Offenbach. All dressed in their best clothes, and even others not so well dressed sang along. All of them including us were dancing in the Place de l'Opera. That night in particular, is one of my loveliest theater memories.

But I could not stop going to the theater. At the Odéon Theater, which is not far from the Jardin de Luxembourg, I continued with the French classics, and listened to them and learnt them over a period of three years. It was a new experience - a gloriously interesting experience.

Lagerstedt

WITH A CHINESE PIGTAIL

While in Paris I preferred to associate with the
French, but I also mixed with people from many
different nations. Thus I often went around with
Asian people just as I did with Negroes, Americans,
Englishmen, Germans and others. I even had a lot to
do with Persians and Arabs. As a rule I used to go
and dine at a restaurant which was near Panthéon.
It was a Greek-Turkish restaurant, where many
Moslems had a meal. I had strange but good food and
found excellent friends there among all those people.
What was most interesting for me actually was to
meet Chinese and Arabs. These Chinese were highly
cultured, and many of them came with me when I
followed Flammarion's lectures at the Sorbonne.
They were dressed in the old fashioned manner with
long braids. I also had Arab friends who astonished
me. Every time I talked with them, I received a
bouquet of words in reply. There is no nation which

can express itself so marvelously as the Arabs. Then Arabia is the land of story-tellers too, but it is also the land of mathematicians. It is after all the Arabs who have pursued mathematics the furthest in the world. They are also the nation of male social life - they can sit up a whole night smoking their hookahs and telling their stories endlessly. And it is marvelous to listen to them.

Among my Chinese friends there was one who was extremely poor. One day he came in and asked me in his peculiar way - the Chinese cannot pronounce 'r', you know, but say 'l' instead. He asked me, "May I bollow a few flancs flom you, Milles?" "Oh yes," I replied, "Take a wallet-full." whereafter I tossed it over to him. It was empty. He wondered how we would be able to live that day.

I had the day before planed a plank, and put all the wood shavings in a bucket beside my little stove, to light a fire at some time in the future. Suddenly my friend was standing there looking at those wood-shavings, he picked up a sharp knife - it was a small penknife - and from those round spiral formed shavings he made the most marvelous puppets which moved up and down when they were pressed downwards. They looked as if they were dancing. I took out paint and brushes - I understood immediately what he wanted. Then we got a piece of board ready in which we hammered small nails. We then tied on these painted mobile puppets with a bit of sewing thread. - I had thread because I had to patch my trousers at times. Then we fixed a handle, a stick, under this piece of board with all the puppet-dolls on. We then went down to the boulevards and started selling them and we were really successful.

We continued with this for many months. He dressed me up as a Chinese - I had a long braided pigtail. Even though I was blond and the pigtail black, it did not matter - we kept on selling. I shall never forget when we were able to eat our first proper meal for a long time, with steak, soup and other good things. We almost ate ourselves sick. We sold for months, and became so well known, we two chinese .. We would regularly hear, "Now we are going to take some of these puppets home with us." We kept selling.

His name was Lo. He lived at my place while we manufactured those pretty little puppets, which became more and more Chinese. Lo himself was dressed in silk, in blue silk embroidered with black, and he was an infinitely fine person. How clean he kept his finger nails, how thoroughly he washed, and what food he would sometimes cook for us! It was very strange, but charming.

We had a marvelous time together. I had plenty of money, was eating well, sleeping even better and working tremendously well. Because of him I was introduced to the Chinese culture and philosophy - I read Lao-Tse, who oddly enough had just been translated by a Franco-German who had been working at the Sorbonne.

When my friend had had enough of selling, he planned to go home to his own country, as he wanted to be buried in China - that is the normal thing for the Chinese. One day he was gone.

TWENTY-FIVE PAINTINGS BY RENOIR

My old friend in the claque Georges Lalanne whom I
mentioned earlier, came to my studio one day eager
to help me. "Charles, if you can raise five thousand
Swedish crowns, you can get some splendid Renoirs,
no less than twenty-five paintings by him." Paris was
not at all keen on him at that time and there was a
man who owned twenty-five Renoirs and wished to
sell them for that price.

I loved Renoir. I ran from friend to friend and
approached others whom I knew slightly and tried to
borrow those five thousand Swedish crowns. But
there was no one I saw who believed me and no one
who liked Renoir. I do not want to name any Swedish
names but I approached a very prosperous Swedish
painter living in Paris at the time, and he said, "Are
you crazy, liking Renoir! I mean it is terrible stuff."

Had I owned those Renoirs today I would proudly
have considered them among the best of my entire

collection, which I had brought to Lidingö. But it all came to nothing.

THE WHITE TIE AND TAILS, THE
MINISTERIAL DINNER
AND THE WRIGHT BROTHERS

I had an invitation to visit the Swedish Minister Åkerman. Prince Eugen was coming to Paris. A month before he came, the Minister's wife the Baroness Louise Åkerman wrote to me. She was a charming person, extremely interested in art and was in every way kind to me, as was the Minister. She asked me to come and meet the Prince, who especially had asked to meet me. "But", she wrote, "you must wear a white tie and tails." I had never once in my lifetime worn such a formal coat and had no money to buy one. Also I did not want to rent one - it was extremely difficult to do that.

That is why I went to a tailor in Avenue de Maine, whom I had never seen before, showed him the Swedish letter which he did not understand, explained everything to him and said, "I am a penniless artist. But if you would make a formal tailcoat for me, I promise to pay you all in due time." He said, "I shall make the coat for you and have it ready in time. When I went to get it, it was ready and waiting for me. I took it without paying a sou and went my way. I could have given a wrong address, you know, but he understood that I was honest and gave it to me.

Then I started to walk to the Étoile, where the Swedish Minister lived. On the way something happened that excited me to such a degree that I forgot the dinner and everything else. On every corner there were large posters announcing that the Wright Brothers, Wilbur Wright and the other one, had flown for the first time over the beaches in Northern France and covered twenty-five meters in the air. Paris was most excited. Everyone in Paris stood reading the news on the corners, everybody was discussing. I became so fantastically happy that one could fly - I had read in Leonardo da Vinci's and other books about attempts to get up and fly like a bird. So I completely forgot about going to dinner, to meet the Minister and Prince. Not until two hours later, after I had prayed to God that he would let me live long enough to fly - not until then - did I remember: Oh Lord, I should have been at dinner two hours ago! I walked over there thinking: They will have dined by now. You will have to tell the truth.

But when I arrived at the Embassy, dinner had been delayed. They were all just as overcome as I by the news that Wilbur Wright and his brother had flown twenty-five meters. They talked about nothing else. Seated around the dinner table we discussed what the consequences of all this could be. Marvelous! One did not think of wars, seeing only the possibilities of being able to travel quickly and comfortably in the air. One fantastic dream was followed by another that evening.

A few years ago, when the only living brother Wilbur Wright was in Detroit and held a lecture he said, "Had I known then, what could become of such inventions, I would never have made it public."

It took me many years before I was able to pay for that tail-coat - it was an entire fortune for me. But when I went and paid the last payment, the tailor said to me with a friendly smile, "It is what I have always said, an artist has never cheated me."

AN OCCULT EPISODE

My fiancee was living in Graz in Austria and I was living in Paris. For many years we never saw one another. One hot summer's day during that period I was walking along Boulevard Montparnasse and was about to go home. It was a weekday. Then suddenly I felt the impulse to go down to the book stall set up inside the colonnade around the Odéon Theater. I felt that I should go there and buy a certain book. I went there and found the book, but it was of no interest to me. It was only about machines, special machines. I bought it and had it sent to Graz in Austria. When I came home there was a letter from my fiancee, who wrote about our friend, Dr Julius Stern, who later, several years afterwards, had to take care of me - because of tuberculosis. She asked me to buy that very book for him from Paris and have it sent directly to Graz. I have never forgotten that - it was an extremely odd incident which seemed inexplicable to me, until I got to know Flammarion who spoke a lot about such things.

PUVIS DE CHAVANNES

The first time I met Prince Eugen in Paris, we talked exclusively about Puvis de Chavannes. He was the first innovator of paintings I knew of and he is still admired and respected today. Later on I discovered that he made careful studies of the mosaics hanging in the Vatican. He received his inspiration there. As is usually the case, one always gets inspired somewhere. The most impressive figure, which I still think is the best, is Saint Geneviève, where she is standing on the roof of her house at night, with the moonlight resting over the city of Paris, and the door behind her ajar. Inside there is a candle which lights up the room. Technically these two things, the moonlight from the outside and the candle light from the inside are magnificent. The calmness over it all is glorious. Chavannes had captivated the Prince too, who also thought he was marvelous.

I have never met Chavannes. Actually the only thing I know about him, is that he left home at five o'clock every morning and walked out to Meudon. He did not take the train - he needed the exercise. When the train came, he always stood at the same gate to cross the railway. The person who told me that was the engine-driver, who recognized him standing there every morning at about six o'clock. The train passed by and he then went over the line and walked on to Meudon in the outskirts of Paris, where he had his studio. He worked there until four, then tired he took the train home and was given dinner and rested. He worked hard. He was rich and worked more than most artists. His paintings can be seen everywhere in France and one always becomes delighted, charmed and full of admiration. I believe he has seven paintings at the Panthéon in Paris. The last time I was at the Panthéon I was distressed and sad. The paintings were completely concealed by war monuments standing there in plaster and stone. Whole lanes of very bad monuments inside the building. They were probably only there temporarily - I hope so.

Up in the high and gigantic arch, which forms the dome of the Panthéon, hung a thin plaited iron thread, on which was fastened an enormous ball with a point at the bottom. This ball, hanging in its probably a hundred feet long thread, turned, showing the earth's movement. This ball was tracing an ellipse, which changed in relation to a circle on the floor, where all the twelve hours were marked. It showed the right time perfectly. It was the earth's movement, one of thirtyone, I think.

THE LOTTERY PRIZE

There was a little incident which I witnessed at a restaurant in Paris, in Rue des Lambres. There were paintings done by Chavannes on the walls, describing the story of an American girl, a very childish thing, but the colors were Chavannesque. The lady who owned the restaurant - I do not remember what she was called, most probably Madame Emilie - was tall and slender with an enormous chin. She managed her restaurant wonderfully well. Fresh flowers on the tables every day and the paintings looked good, if one did not look too carefully at them. The whole place was clean and tidy. Her husband was a small swarthy Italian fellow, who had to be at Les Halles every morning at five o'clock to buy the day's food and drag it home in a barrow.

I was sitting there one evening eating alone - the restaurant was not yet full of people. Mostly Englishmen and Americans ate there. I heard then far off how the door to the street opened - there was a long corridor between the entrance and the dining room. Suddenly I heard a terrible cry. I wondered what had happened. I thought I should rush out to see if anyone needed help. But no one did.

It was the little host - and now he came in and shouted, jumping for joy, "C'est moi, c'est, monsieur, who has won the bumper prize, le grand lot." He had won a gigantic sum on the lottery. I cannot remember how much. He then flew out and there was laughter, merriment and shouting, and then he came back to me again. He said, "Yes, well, I bought this ticket before I got married so the money belongs to me!" Afterwards when I was leaving the restaurant everyone had sour faces. He was the only one who seemed to be happy. He was rushing around and did not know what to say or do, just kept on repeating, "C'est moi, it belongs to me, it does not belong to you!" and that was his wife he was referring to. The result was that there was a terrible quarrel and a divorce. They sold the restaurant. She received a bit of money from him afterwards, but that was the end of the delightful restaurant, which ceased to exist.

There you see what money can do to people.

THE THEFT OF MONA LISA

Once at a restaurant in Paris I met a man who sat down at the same table. We became good friends. I do not remember his name, but he spun a good tale about what he had done when he visited the Louvre. When the closing gongs sounded he jumped into a gigantic terracotta pot. As soon as the guard came by he crouched inside. No one thought of anyone being able to hide in there.

He was a journalist and did this especially to test the security guards in the Louvre. He witnessed two security patrols during the night. The guards of course did not look in any direction, but walked and talked with their lanterns in their hands. Later, in the morning, when he mingled with the public someone came up to him and said, "How did you get in? You cannot be up here so early without having passed by down below. It always takes time to get here." Then he added, "Now come with me, we shall go to the superintendent." The journalist introduced himself to the superintendent and told him what he had done. There was a great commotion of course. Probably as a result of this the Louvre became better guarded. Anyone could have gone there and taken something.

As you know, 'La Gioconda' by Leonardo da Vinci hangs there and true enough it was stolen later. During Mussolini's time the curator of the great gallery in Florence got a letter from a man who said, "I am the one who stole the painting from the Louvre. If you promise not to mention it to anyone, I shall put it back." The curator promised. Up came a little man - I think he was a smith. He showed the painting to him. It was the da Vinci canvas which had been cut from the frame at the Louvre. The curator then said, "It will not be possible to keep this a secret, as it is such a valuable article. There could be trouble, indeed political trouble. I must report this." The man and the curator both went to Rome. He was asked. "Why did you steal this?" "Well, I consider it one of the world's finest paintings. It is an Italian who painted it, and I want it to be in Italy." Purely patriotic reasons. Well now, according to what I heard, the man was given a prison sentence, but he was secretly released the day after. The news that he had been sentenced was made official in the newspapers. The whole world was satisfied, but when he was freed - the world knew nothing about that.

It was a delightful event when the painting came back to Paris. The whole of Paris' Art Corps, no matter which group they belonged to, were down at the Gare de Lyon with large wagons filled with flowers. Her own wagon - La Gioconda's wagon, in which she was enthroned - was slowly brought back, with music playing, to the Louvre. This has always appealed to me, in France there is an understanding between companions and a readiness to help, that is wonderful. It is a paradise as far as art is concerned. In the summer many Frenchman come to Lidingö in order to see the little I have collected here. It is marvelous to hear them talk about art, and how necessary they consider art to be.

Lagerstedt

I was in Paris during the Dreyfus affair. I followed the press, observed the people and witnessed an extraordinary interesting but also rather unhappy time.

The first person who acquainted me with the situation was my concierge - in France the concierges are the ones who actually know everything that goes on. They know all about the inmates of the houses and courtyards. I have been told that when policemen need to know something about strangers or non-strangers they always go to the concierge. The strange thing is that if you are not born in Paris, even a Frenchman living in Paris, is always étranger - a foreigner. I have heard this so often, "Ah, c'est un étranger." So naturally I got into trouble with my concierge at Rue de la Grande Chaumière. One day at the beginning of my stay, he came and asked me, "D'ou venez-vous, monsieur? Est-ce que vous êtes

Prussien?" - Where do you come from, Sir, are you Prussian? - "No, I am a Swede." He had no idea what a Swede was. Then he said after looking at me for a while, "Vous êtes Prussien tout de même." - You are a Prussian nevertheless.

Afterwards this man and I became very good friends, although he was very difficult to get on with. He had two sons with whom I became good friends. I cycled with them out in the country. He had a wife, an old women, who was extremely fine and amiable and softened him up a bit. I left the studio, after being there for six years, because they slaughtered my lovely cat, who had slept in my bed. They hung his fur on the door. It was not funny to see the cat's fur hanging on the door and even less so considering their reason for slaughtering the cat. A cat is not tasty if it gets too old. It is rather odd to see that sort of thing occurring in Germany and in other countries too. Many times when one has eaten at cheap restaurants, one has found bits of cat's claws and whiskers in the meat soup. As you know, one gets used to everything in the end.

Anyway the concierge was the first person to start pumping me about what I thought of Dreyfus. I did not really know exactly what the whole matter was about before he gave me the newspapers. He was indeed very familiar with the whole matter and studied it as did everyone at the time - everyone was for or against, but most were against the poor man who was harassed so terribly. He became known, you know, because he was said to have sold secret state documents, army documents, to another country. There was a tribunal and he was condemned to Devil's Island, where he was chained to his bed, and walked with shackles around his arms and legs, which were never seen too or even taken off. I have seen poor animals in zoological gardens treated in such a way, with their legs bleeding, and this has upset me. Actually it is even harder for them, as they cannot speak or communicate - but probably one could not do that on Devil's Island either.

I set about studying the matter and followed it closely, understood it first when I had read the newspaper l'Aurore with Zola's marvelous article 'J'accuse'. It was like being lit up suddenly by a flash of lightning. That a human could be treated in that way when no one knew for certain if he was guilty or not! When I read his reply at the tribunal, it was clear to me that he was innocent. When I heard Colonel Piccard, who was arrested himself and put in prison for defending Zola's article and Dreyfus, I became even more certain and it was even more interesting to follow. Then there was Laborie, the Lawyer! How he fought for him, that poor man, whom they had taken from his family and kept imprisoned for five years on that infernal island, north of Venezuela, on the cliffs where there was no vegetation, just sun and misery. I have heard sea-captains say, "You love the sun, but I know people who hate it." One can get too much of it, and that was just how it was there. Fugitives have escaped by swimming across the sea and in turn wrestling with the many sharks. Those who escaped the sharks have become feeble-minded afterwards.

There was something odd about this matter, as it not only stirred up the whole of Paris, but also France and the whole world, in particular it concerned each one of us. I have never been racially prejudiced, or thought of anything suggesting that one race should be inferior to another. For me the differences have always been between man and man, woman and woman, how their intelligence and goodness of heart have collaborated. I am not fond of those who are only intelligent and also those who are only good. It is our historian from Uppsala, Erik Gustaf Geijer, who wrote a long time ago: To be good is easy enough. It is so easy to find good people who can do all sorts of things without thinking, but the most important thing in the world is to think, even when one is good.

I went to visit Colonel Piccard, to shake his hand and thank him for what he wrote. When he was interviewed there was never any complaint about his condition. He said, "I am content, I am quite all right." He never said a word about how he felt, sitting in his gloomy cell and not being able to meet anyone - least of all me. I was a foreigner and had no real right to visit such a man. Laborie, the lawyer, was shot in the lungs, but survived. Likewise he did not falter afterwards. Then there was Zola. He ran away, when he should have paid a gigantic sum as penalty for what he had written in l'Aurore. He took off for London and stayed there with his wife. Later he died in Paris because he failed to shut the heaters doors. The gas came into the room at night, suffocating him to death.

When I was able to get away from my work, I would walk around Paris to get small glimpses of the city. I visited the press, where all the newspapers of the city were printed. - I do not remember the name of the street. To enable all the newspapers to be printed regularly these immense printing presses ran none stop. I saw them. Fantastic! There was a terrific whirring of machines and buzzing of people dashing around. Just across from the press, in the street, was a restaurant, which gave me something to think about. There sat all those ideological enemies, eating their lunches or suppers in peace and quiet. There they sat, those people who during the day crossfired one another with words - eating in peace and quiet just like good friends. It taught me a lesson - always remember that we humans are constantly fighting for various ideals. It would probably be a really bad state of affairs indeed, if we all agreed on everything, we would really be in a mess then. It was a bacteriologist, who proved that if one has a glass of stagnant water, then that water will rot quite soon, especially if it is placed out in the sun. But if one stirs it with a glass rod, moving the water violently then one may drink it without danger.

Being a spectator at this restaurant, where it was calm and quiet, everyone eating at peace with one another despite different ideals, was something I liked enormously.

Well the case continued and Dreyfus was to appear before a new court. It was at Rennes where he would once again be tried. He was not acquitted (after spending five years on Devil's Island) but pardoned - forgiven - by Loubet, the new President. So now tempers were stirred up again on account of him to have him condemned again. It was very odd to see the frenzy with my own eyes. One morning as I came into the street - Rue de la Grande Chaumière - and walked up towards Boulevard Montparnasse, I found those streets jammed with tents and bivouac fires and soldiers. It was feared that there would be a revolution in France. I went on down to the Tuilerie gardens. All the wrought iron gates were closed and inside prisoners lived for three days and two nights out in the open air - it was warm and fine but even so they had to sleep as best they could. The prisoners were people who the authorities feared would cause trouble. I went along with some French friends to Bois de Boulogne, to the first Longchamps' competition - trotting race - which Loubet would attend as President. Everything went peacefully. There was such a crowd that we never arrived at Longchamps but instead lay there on the lawn and waited to see what would happen and who would win the prize and so forth. It was a marvelous day. Then suddenly a rumor began to spread that something had happened to Loubet at Longchamps, but no one knew what. After a while the Les Gardes Républicains came by - a whole corps of mounted police, soldiers and officers on horseback - with beautiful uniforms and long ponytails on their helmets. There was a deadly silence among the crowd. They held the reins in their left hand and a revolver in their other hand. They shot passed us riding out to Longchamps. Half an hour later we saw Loubet's landau, in which he sat alone, driving the same way back in deadly silence. The whole of the landau was covered yellow with eggs, and so was he. It was ghastly though interesting to see how far people can get carried away when they are upset.

I shall never forget the day when Dreyfus was to be pardoned. It was to be announced in Paris, sometime between four and half past four. I walked out into the street where everyone was walking around waiting. The camelots, who sold newspapers came rushing from the center. They had bundles of newspapers to sell. They held each bundle under their left arm and with their right hand they took out a newspaper, folded it up in the air and handed it to the purchaser, at the same moment taking the money. A perfect variety number which they had learnt. They chased around as if their lives were at stake, calling out the newspapers. People bought them wildly. I ended up by walking alone down the boulevards and streets. No transport, buses or trams. Everything was silent except in the cafes and restaurants where they rejoiced, and church bells rang throughout Paris -

because he had been convicted again. He was not even pardoned but was convicted again. But in the end he was pardoned by Loubet who did as he had intended.

I have never forgotten that moment and never shall forget it as there was something terrible about seeing people ranting and raving. They were now inside the cafes, celebrating in a frenzy of joy about the poor man who was convicted back to Devil's Island. But he never went back. Loubet became very impopular because of the pardon. He was an unusually courageous man.

I went to Zola's house just when all his things were to be sold to pay the debt he owed the state or court or whatever it was. It was packed with people. I only came as far as the front of his flat, which was filled with works of art and souvenirs. People walked around there saying that they were going to buy this and that, and have this and that. The usual ruthless urge which the human race has. His publishers bought a cheap simple dining table for the total debt, and the others left the apartment disappointed.

Then when Dreyfus came home - I went to the place where he lived - hoping to shake his hand. I only got to see him from a distance and he looked shocking. Wretched, broken. I never got close enough to him, as there were many who wanted to shake his hand, especially those among his closest friends. Later, as we all know, he was reinstated into the army with a high rank. He was decorated once more with the medals that had previously been torn from his uniform in front of his own soldiers. So now he was reinstated in the army. After that he lived for quite a long time.

154

AS AN UNINVITED GUEST AT A CASTLE

In the summer when I had the money, I used to ride my bicycle through France. I loved it and experienced many interesting things, as one always does in France. The people there are so friendly, provided one is not suspected of being a spy or something like that, which often happened in those days.

Now it so occured that I had been looking at Mont St Michel in northern France in Brittany - and intended to ride back to the place where I had rented a room to have a bath and refresh myself.

The heaven then opened. It rained cats and dogs. I had no shelter. I was riding through a forest, a pitch black forest, and could finally not see a thing. Night fell, it got dark and I cycled on, not finding a way out - the forest seemed endless. Then I passed a little by-road. I saw a light burning in the distance. I turned in there and came to a large castle surrounded by moats. A castle which was built in the eighteenth century. One moat was filled with water, a drawbridge had been lowered so one could walk to the entrance. This was an enormous castle. I saw a little light - obviously the caretaker's light. I knocked at the door, in which a hatch opened and I observed a women's face - very ugly and angry. "Who is it?" she asked. I answered, "I have lost my way and request permission to stay the night out of this storm." The little door closed. Well I knocked again and then a man's face appeared. I explained the same thing to him. He was less afraid and opened the door for me and let me take my bicycle in. I had to wring the water out of my clothes, and I was directed to lie down under the lowest part of a hugh staircase where it looked as if dogs had slept. There was a piece of rag on the stone floor and that was where I had to lie. I did not lie down - I was up walking all night in that great hall where there were seven stuffed wolves, all of which seemed to rush at me when I came in.

The day after, I was told that this castle was called Chanteloup - Wolf Song - that it was situated in a huge forest and that the owner of the castle lived in Southern France and had not been there for forty years. In the morning I fell asleep. It is strange that I did not catch a cold. I was awakened by the caretakers offering me hot café au lait and a little sandwich, in their kitchen. Half an hour later we were good friends. They were sorry they had given me such a bad place, but as I was so wet they could not do otherwise. We had a pleasant time, dried my clothes in front of a stove and I was allowed to walk around the old castle and look at all the remarkable things. Everything was very old. Large giantsize beds, old paintings, old objects wherever I went. By lunch we were such good friends that I was not permitted to travel on but to stay and rest. I was given soup and marvelous food. Then when I was about to leave in the afternoon, they insisted that I stayed - I was to sleep in one of those giantsized beds up in the palace somewhere. I stayed but thought it was haunted the whole night. I kept waking up, thinking I heard footsteps and voices. Actually I was somewhat shaken, but in the morning I wakened and stayed another day resting and then rode home to Grandeville. I corresponded with these two old people for some time afterwards.

Much later I read about a conspiracy against Napoleon. I have read about Napoleon many times, being extremely interested in the man's life. He was to be murdered. All the conspirators hid in that same castle with the moats around, and plotted his assassination. However they were all caught by the minister of police whose name was Fouchet, from whose descendants we have the d'Otrante family in Sweden. So there was never any attempt on Napoleon's life thanks to Fouchet's swift intervention.

THE HERMIT AT AUVERGNE

Another time I was hiking up in the hills of Auvergne. I stayed down in a little hamlet, where I ate together with friendly families. They never trusted any bank, instead it was always Grandma - the old woman - who looked after the family's money, which she buried in a place only she knew - this procedure is still customary there today.

In the distance I had seen a black hole somewhere in the hills. They told me that a hermit lived there. I really wanted to see that hermit. It was hard work climbing up the slopes of the hill, but I found him. When I reached him, he was sitting in front of the cave, where he lived. He smiled at me. He had watched me for quite a while. I had passed a great many small farms on the way. He offered me fresh milk at once. He herded cattle up there and was a fine friendly man. When I entered the cave I saw many fine books. Academical books about most of the sciences. I asked him, "Where exactly do you come from? Do you read things like this?" Yes indeed, he had been a professor at a university which I promised never to name. I never got to know his name.

I stayed there for three days. He baked his own bread. He got other things from the farms down in the valley. Milk, of course, he got from the cows. He was paid and made his living from herding the cattle. He detested war and did not like the modern attitude towards education. He lived up there isolated from people. He was one of the most wonderful men I have met in my life. He was not married and lived like a perfect bachelor with his two dogs. The children came up from the farms and played with the tame animals he had there. I have portrayed this man in the bronze group which is to be erected in Washington's new cemetery. There he sits watching - full of surprise - while a boy and a girl are playing with birds, lizards and the like.

Each year I travelled down and visited him. We always had a pleasant time together. I stayed longer and longer each time. The last time I went there I stopped at a farm to get my breath back and to rest. They then told me that one day he had come down to them, bought something and told them that both his dogs were buried. A few days later he was dead himself. People who had gone up there found him dead in his bed. He had committed suicide. He did not want to return to civilization, which he called 'uncivilization'.

IN A SPANISH PRISON

I was riding my bicycle - still on my own - south towards the Pyrenees and Spain. I came to a little town - without knowing it I had obviously passed some sort of border, where one was not allowed to pass without showing one's passport. Two policemen came along the road. On my right rose the snowy tops of the Pyrenees and ahead of me was a little town which looked delightfully inviting. Both those policemen stopped me and asked to see my passport. At that time nobody needed a passport in France, or anywhere else in Europe - in 1914 a law was introduced, compelling everyone to carry passports.

I took out a tenancy agreement and handed it to one of them. I was rather relieved to notice that he held it upside down. Obviously he could not read. Then a third policeman came along. He snatched the contract out of his colleague's hands, looked at him scornfully, said nothing but turned it the right way up, read it and said, "This is a tenancy contract." "Yes, I have nothing else," I said. I happened to have it with me. It was from 106 Boulevard Montparnasse in Paris. Anyway they asked me to follow them. I was put in prison, the most marvelous prison in the world. Around the yard were colonnades, old Gothic ones - it was obviously an old monastery. To the right we still had the Pyrenees with their snowy tops. Inside on one side of the immense yard stood a gigantic tree. I was then given my little cell with a bench to lie on and water to drink.

Shortly before twelve o'clock one of the policemen came to me - I was the only prisoner they had - and invited me to lunch under that gigantic tree. A table was built around the trunk and there were benches to sit on. I was given a delightful lunch which the wife of one of the policemen had cooked. After coffee they took out playing cards, and I, who had never been used to playing cards, learnt a Spanish-French game that afternoon. At about five o'clock I won some pesos from them! I felt very clever. At six o'clock the announcement for my release came from the Swedish Legation, but by that time we were so delighted with

166

each other that I asked to stay the night. So I slept there. That was that amusing little meeting.

REFLECTIONS IN ROME

When the sun is shining there is scarcely nothing more magnificent than to see the view from Janicolo. The city in its wonderful, so to speak, diluted colors. Here there are no glaring colors on the houses or facade paint but instead everything is completely in tone, which makes the houses and streets blend into a sensitive and fine symphony of colors. Paris has something of this too - especially when one looks at Paris from the Eiffel Tower - one becomes surprised over the simplicity of the color choice. I have often thought of that when I look at the hard and glaring colors used in Sweden, particularly in Stockholm - venetian blinds in a dazzling red. Appalling raw color compositions.

Even when buildings in Rome are restored, attempts are always made to give the buildings beautiful colors and it's done with immense delicacy and feeling, which one does not find in any other nation. One may compare Innsbruck for example, where there are medieval streets and where all the modern houses have been painted in different ways. It is very picturesque and pretty, but it destroys the total feeling, the feeling of wholeness. Here in Rome the architecture cooperates with the entire piazza.

When arriving in Rome one of my first steps has always been to go down into St Peter's basement, so to speak - to the crypt. A women is lying buried there among all the Popes. It is our Queen Kristina. I am probably one of the few Swedes who has always placed four candles on her coffin, I have done that for years. Each time I go there the priests recognize me and I receive my candles without saying anything. I have a certain admiration for her. Once I came to a monastery in the south of Rome, where the prior conducted us foreigners around - he had no idea that I was Swedish - he told us that Queen Kristina had lived there for half a year, just to study the library. That lady, he said, spoke seventeen languages fluently. You know, when he said that I had to believe it. It is fantastic. Once in Paris I met a man who could speak even more languages, due to his profession. She did it purely out of love for history and science.

Another thing which I always did when I came to

Rome in the fall was to buy myself a bag of grapes and sit down late in the evening by one of the two great fountains in St Peter's Square and look up at the Pope's apartment in the Vatican to see when he went to bed - the lights were put out then, you see. Small games like that amuse me. If one thinks back to the time when great gilded glass coaches with aristocrats and royalty passed the Trevia Fountain, one cannot understand how they could have driven there. It is very difficult even now for cars to enter there. But of course nobody wants the fountain to be removed.

AN ART CRITIC

A man I met in Sweden once came up to me one day at a restaurant and said, "What do you think of this dreadful fountain?" "Dreadful, you say?" I replied, "I think it is one of the most wonderful things to look at." "You think this fountain is beautiful, I think it's rubbish. Just look how those horses are made. There are nothing but faults in it all." "Listen my dear fellow," I said, "You are so and so many years old, been writing about art the whole of your life, and still have not reached the point where you realize that it is precisely those so called faults, so different from the academical dry and dead, which will keep this fountain admired for all times.

Fountains are noisy and splash... That is precisely what I have heard many times in Sweden. "You will have to make sure that the water does not run out on to the square as well." Then I would reply that on the continent - particularly in Italy and France - there are usually great pools in the direction of the wind. That is what is so charming about it. In Rome the water comes from up in the hills around Tivoli. There are enormous waterfalls, partly used for the scenery, and partly for practical purposes - electricity.

When you place a sculpture in the open air it is important that there are no cavities underneath. It should be flat and strongly built. Also you should keep the anatomy simple.

I am always telling young people, whether they have been in Sweden or elsewhere, that they should disregard working too much in detail with the model and anatomy. They should think of the Chinese who use sculptures exclusively as ornaments. Even if one wants to give them a spiritual content, they are first and foremost ornaments. I know how I usually feel myself. One should know one's anatomy so well, without thinking about it. That is to say, know the technique, and the different techniques in stone and bronze, as they differ greatly from one another. In our day and age we know that the Greeks worked mostly in bronze and did their copies in marble. Previously I thought it was the other way around. The Chinese have done most of their sculptures in bronze, but they have also carved grand works out of stone, and there they have simplified the forms enormously. No nation has just wild and free forms, flying in the wind, as the Chinese.

When I sit in a crowded restaurant, I think of an episode that happened to Goethe. His good friend Herder - the philologist - wrote to him, "I want to meet you to talk about the German Language. Let us meet at a restaurant where we can sit and enjoy ourselves." They went to a restaurant, and spoke a long while. Suddenly a group of young officers came rushing into the restaurant and sat down at the table beside them. They had obviously been having a good time and wanted to continue. They drank a great deal of wine and became so noisy that Goethe and Herder were unable to continue their conversation. Then Goethe took a little scrap of paper out of his pocket and wrote as follows:

Wasser allein macht stumm
das beweisen in Wasser die Fische
Wein allein macht dumm
das beweisen die Herren am Tische
Da ich keines von beiden will sein
ich mische mit Wasser mein Wein

Water alone makes you dumb
the fishes in the water prove that

Wine alone makes one foolish
this is shown by the men at the table
Since I neither want to be dumb or foolish
I mix my wine with water

Goethe improvised in this charming way and sent the
note to the next table!

AN AMERICAN EDUCATOR

It is my impression that one meets most idealists in America. I have lived and worked in eleven countries altogether, as a craftsman, artist etc. I have never met so many true idealists as in America. To name one of them only, I would like to tell you a little about Floyd Star. Floyd Star is an old man now, and he came to me a few years ago, asking me to sell a bronze picture, portraying some remarkable man in the Bible. I suggested that he should have my sketch, which I had once done in St Paul's. Paulus, while bolts of lightning are flashing around him, and his horse is rearing, he bends backward with his hand in front of his face. It was God who was speaking. Floyd Star was terribly pleased with that, and I gave it to him in bronze - he never needed to pay for it. I loved that man. I have kept in contact with him for a long time by sending him a contribution to his work - a minor sum, a five or ten crown note, or whatever I can manage in dollars once a year - according to the same system as when one sends contributions to Father Flanagan, who lives in the West. They both have as their mission in life to take care of young boys whom they try to save from hardships. Now we shall stay with Floyd Star. He has dedicated his life to saving boys, who have been taken by the police, and who are going to be punished for one thing or another, rash things. We all know how boys are, after all. I expect all of us men have been rash, and done things which later on in life we may even have been ashamed of. We have felt a little unsure of ourselves when we have noticed that we have not given enough thought to what we were doing. Floyd Star's approach was that whenever any boy - wherever he may be in the States - had been taken by the police, he went there and tried to dissuade the police from taking disciplinary action. Sometimes he had great difficulty in getting the boy in question to the Institute, which he himself started. He started very gradually in a small scale, and now it is a large institution where he himself is the life and soul of the place. All the boys call him 'Uncle Floyd'. He has carried out this work for many years now, and 96-98 percent of the boys have become the best citizens in the States. They are in charge of large insurance companies or have positions of trust in Washington. Once a year they always meet at Uncle Floyd's, of course! It was their own idea, he never asked them to.

When he comes to us he usually sits and tells us about his experiments with these boys. Once he got a boy who was terribly hard to handle. He was hard and swore dreadfully. Floyd mentioned the fact that he was building a church for the boys. "I don't need that, I don't belong to God. I belong to the devil," the boy said. " I want to be an angel with the devil, when I die. He hasn't any angels, so I am going to be one and help him." Floyd, a wise man, let him have his way. He thought: I will probably get on well with him one day.

One day he noticed that the boy was deeply fond of a work of art, which was there. He told him, "If you promise not to swear for three months, I shall give you that." The boy stared at him and looked at the work of art. He stood a long time admiring it, and afterwards Floyd never heard him swear again. But the promise was to be kept for three months, and one day just before those three months has passed, he comes into Uncle Floyd and says, "Uncle Floyd, I swore today. But I only half-swore." Then Floyd already knew that he had him on his side. "Well, what was the course of it?" he wondered. "Well, you know you told me to see to the horses. I did, but one horse trod on my foot. You know how that felt. I swore, but I only half-swore." Floyd smiled, he knew, "Now I have him and am making a decent man out of him." He gave him the gift in advance.

Another example was a boy who was impossible to manage. His father had committed murder, murdered his wife and the boy's brothers and sisters, but the boy had escaped in some extraordinary way. He was very hard that boy. He dreamed all the time of meeting his father, (when he found out he had a father), though he did not know that his father had been condemned to life imprisonment and hard labor. He absolutely wanted to meet his father and asked Uncle Floyd where he was. Finally he found out that he was in prison. He was even told that his father, who was illiterate, had murdered his mother, brothers and sisters out of despair one day.

Nevertheless the boy still wanted to see his father. He idolized him in his imagination. One day Floyd took him to visit his father, although it was a long journey. In prison his father had learnt to read and write, to work with books and acquire knowledge. He improved and took one examination after the other in prison and finally got a Ph.D. He thought that what he had done before was something terrible and appalling, but felt that he was basically innocent, as at the time he had not understood what he was doing. He did not know what was good or bad at that time. The authorities were very accommodating towards him. He was given a room to study in at the prison, where he studied earnestly. When his son left the prison after visiting his father, he was told that his father was going to be released. He would go out into life as a learned man. That is the story. His father is dead now, but as long as he lived, father and son kept together as the best of friends.

Another story he told me was about a boy who stole cars. The police chased him and caught him and kept him a long time. But Floyd soon got him out to his Institution thinking, "I shall make a man out of him." Then as bad luck would have it, the boy stole cars there as well. The chief of police chased him and a whole line of police cars were after him and caught him. Floyd was there too. While the police and Floyd and everybody were standing there talking, the boy sneaked away and stole the car belonging to the Chief of Police. He took off at great speed. He was chased again and finally tumbled into a ditch. Fortunately he did not get hurt. Well, that was that boy's youthful error, but now he too is one of the most eminent men in the country.

I have experienced something of that sort in England too, where a father got to know of his son's crime. He said to him quite calmly one day. "Yes, you ought to be ashamed of that. But I am glad that it is done, as you now will not do any more." That was the case. I am all for allowing boys to let off steam, if they need to, providing there is a strong hand to take care of them, and make them into the best of men. I have seen so much of that sort of thing in my lifetime.

Floyd Star's Home for Boys, where he takes care of an infinite number of boys, is one of the finest things in America. There are many men and women who devote their time to similar tasks, but Floyd Star is probably the foremost of them all.

THE ELEVATOR OPERATOR WHO
LOVED ITALY

The hotel where we usually stay, my wife and I, when we are in New York, is called The Plaza and is situated near Central Park. It is an old Italian hotel, immensely big and splendidly built. The people there are extremely friendly and kind. My friends always think that I own the entire hotel, as I know every single person there.

In that hotel there is an elevator operator, an Irishman, old and ugly but with a wonderful expression in his eyes. He stands eight to ten hours a day, elevating people, who all look at him quickly and indifferently. But once we had a talk together, when there was nobody in the elevator. I sat down on a bench inside the large elevator, which seats twenty people. Then he started talking about Italy. I noticed that he knew a lot about Italy, so I thought that he had probably been reading a book, about Italy.

The last time I stayed at the hotel, I went to the elevator where he used to stand. He was not there. I went to the next one; he was nowhere to be found. I inquired about his whereabouts; no one knew. Four months later he was standing by the elevator, the usual old place where he had stood for years. I asked him if he had been ill. "No," he said, "I have not been ill, but I came back from Italy last night. I started work today. I flew." "Italy?" I said. "You have talked of that before. Do you travel to Italy?" "Yes, every other year. I save up so that I can travel to Italy and live there for eight months. I live at the best hotels, eat marvelous food, drink splendid wine and the rest of the time I am in various cities looking at the wonderful things, created by the Italians, so I know the whole of Italy, from north to south.

To hear this poor elevator boy talk about Padua, Donatello's statue of Gattamelata or hear him talk of Colleoni in Venice by Verocchio or about the statue of Marcus Aurelius at the Campodoglio or the buildings in Florence, Ravenna, Venice, Rome, Naples - he has seen everything more than once. "Well, what about your wife then? You told me once you were married." "Yes I am. I leave her at home; she does not like art. She plays cards and drinks in the evening, and then she is content. Sits with her friends, playing cards, that satisfies her, so I travel alone. I have a wonderful time."

Back in Sweden I received letters from him. They are the most beautiful letters I have ever received. How could he express himself so well? - An Irishman, born in Ireland, earning his living by standing in an elevator, and yet a truly learned man.

BOTTICELLI AND THE CAB-DRIVER

I was going to Brooklyn Museum in New York. I never really liked taking the subway so I took a cab, though it was a long way to drive. It was a glorious spring day. It was midday as we drove through the Italian quarters. There I noticed how the driver was steering - he was constantly looking to the right. There on the sidewalk a beautiful girl was walking along, dressed just like Botticelli's Spring. She tripped along in her pretty flowery dress, and he sat mostly looking at her. So I said to him, "Driver, drive slowly. I like that girl too."

He drove slowly and the road was long. When we arrived at Brooklyn's gigantic museum, he did not leave but said, "I shall stay till you are finished here." To that I said, "No, drive home as I shall probably stay here a few hours." It doesn't matter, I shall put the taxi meter off." When I came out, quite a long time later, he was standing there. Then I sat down beside him, and we talked the entire time about art, about Botticelli's glorious 'Springs', of which one sees so many in these districts. The whole journey was like a midsummer day, an experience, with the driver an Italian who had been in America for seven years. There wasn't any chance of him accepting money from me. It was after all seventeen dollars. But I arranged things in a better way for him. Since then I have met that man many times. He lives with his mother in New York.

Another time a taxi driver happened to see that I was tired. He stopped his cab and said, "Climb in here and I shall drive you home." He drove me to the hotel. He then said to me, "You can live at this hotel, but you should not eat here." "I know," I said, "I eat at other places." "Come home with me. We are newly-weds and have a little baby." I went with him, and had a magnificent supper, and his wife - quite charming - was the best of cooks. I have been there several times since. But during the last war he disappeared.

Meeting such people, simple, splendid people is an experience of adventure.